INTERNET E-MAIL
QUICK TOUR

SENDING, RECEIVING & MANAGING YOUR MESSAGES ONLINE

TED ALSPACH

VENTANA PRESS

Internet E-Mail Quick Tour: Sending, Receiving & Managing Your Messages Online
Copyright © 1995 by Ted Alspach

Library of Congress Cataloging-in-Publication Data

Alspach, Ted.
    Internet E-mail quick tour : sending, receiving and
managing your messages online / Ted Alspach.
       p. cm.
    Includes index.
    ISBN 1-56604-220-8
    I. Title
TK5105.875.I57A438   1995
651.7--dc20   95-1924
                                  CIP

Book design: Marcia Webb
Cover design: Dawne Sherman
Index service: Dianne Bertsch, Answers Plus
Technical review: Gary Moore
Design staff: Dawne Sherman, Marcia Webb
Editorial staff: Angela Anderson, Walter R. Bruce III, Paula Edelson, Eric Edstam,
    Tracye Giles, Tim C. Mattson, Clif McCormick, Pam Richardson
Production staff: John Cotterman, Dan Koeller, Lance Kozlowski
Proofreader: Martin V. Minner

First Edition 9 8 7 6 5 4 3 2 1
Printed in the United States of America

Ventana Press, Inc.
P.O. Box 2468
Chapel Hill, NC 27515
919/942-0220
FAX 919/942-1140

Limits of Liability and Disclaimer of Warranty
The author and publisher of this book have used their best efforts in preparing the book and the programs contained in it. These efforts include the development, research and testing of the theories and programs to determine their effectiveness. The author and publisher make no warranty of any kind, expressed or implied, with regard to these programs or the documentation contained in this book.

    The author and publisher shall not be liable in the event of incidental or consequential damages in connection with, or arising out of, the furnishing, performance or use of the programs, associated instructions and/or claims of productivity gains.

TRADEMARKS

ABOUT THE AUTHOR

Ted Alspach is author of *The Macworld Illustrator 5.0/5.5 Bible* (IDG Books), *The Complete Idiot's Guide to QuarkXPress* and *The Complete Idiot's Guide to Photoshop* (both published by Alpha Books). As the owner of Bezier, a Macintosh training company in Scottsdale, Arizona, Ted has been training users in desktop publishing, graphics, and Macintosh- and Windows-based computers since 1988. Ted is the creator of Lefty Casual and Ransom Note, two popular shareware fonts that have appeared in several publications and logos. In addition to these activities, Ted also spends his time as an America Online Forum consultant.

ACKNOWLEDGMENTS

First, thanks to my mom, who inspired me to write this book as she tried valiantly to communicate with me via Internet e-mail across the country. Her questions and enthusiasm drove this project to get started, and helped shape it into the handy little guide you have before you.

A grateful thanks to Jen for (1) bearing with me as I spent entire days online, tying up the fax/modem line (we'll have four phone lines soon to prevent future problems and my imminent death by strangulation), (2) for feeding me and the kids when I was immersed in writing this book, (3) for letting me watch *American Gladiators* (part of me thinks she likes it as well), and (4) for trying valiantly to communicate with me via Internet e-mail across the house.

Thanks to the kids, especially Tools, whose name I've been using online for years. All he wanted in return was a sidebar in a book, so here it is (see Chapter 2).

A hearty thanks to ICSRob@aol.com, DRichards@crl.com, SandeeC@aol.com, 75431.1752@Compuserve.com, AMPDarlene@eWorld.com, Bigiduz@davidson.edu, DSolomon@eWorld.com, AFLGeneS@aol.com, Sfranks@panix.com, FortuneH@crl.com, ErikPaul@aol.com, 73221.1705@Compuserve.com, Spiker@eWorld.com, SLSC@eWorld.com, SreeIntr@aol.com, MRoney@aol.com and all the other individuals with whom my primary contact is through Internet e-mail.

Even more thanks go to those individuals who got new Internet e-mail addresses while I was writing this book, including KWhopper@aol.com, 72994.1293@Compuserve.com, MMiller@eWorld.com, DLoRez@aol.com, HBGcrplimo@eWorld.com, NancyArt@aol.com, PatAcad@aol.com and Freddie23@aol.com. Not only are they friends, they're research as well.

Finally, a special thanks to everyone at Ventana Press who was involved with this project, especially Walt Bruce, Pam Richardson, Paula Edelson, Eric Edstam, Tim Mattson, John Cotterman and Marcia Webb.

CONTENTS

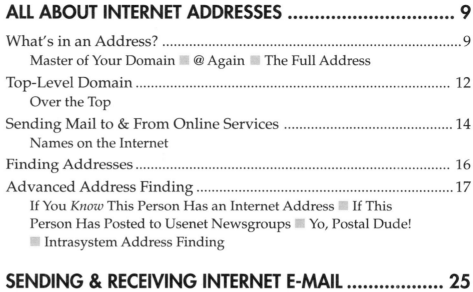

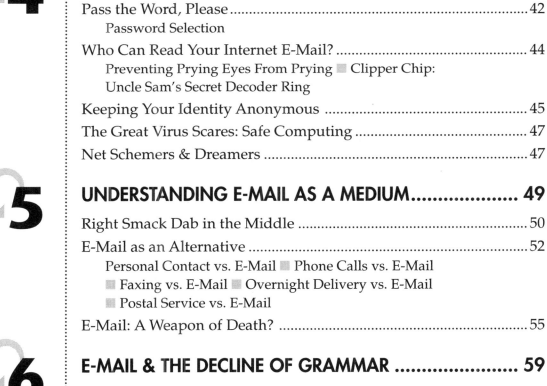

10 BEYOND E-MAIL 101

INTRODUCTION

I think it was my wife who said that I write so much e-mail on the Internet that I could fill up a book with it. Of course, she really didn't mean a book *about* e-mail, which is what this book ended up being. And this particular book didn't stop me from writing e-mail; on the contrary, it actually egged me on to new levels of Net-life that I could access by e-mail.

Internet e-mail is becoming a new cornerstone of electronic society. Much as the telephone has made the world fewer than 13 digits away (unless you have MCI, in which case add on about 300 extra numbers just to call from a pay phone), the Internet provides an easy way for anyone with an e-mail address to be reached "through the Net." More and more people and companies are getting connected, and many of these people don't quite know what to do once they're plugged in. Add to that the millions of subscribers to America Online, CompuServe, Prodigy, etc., and others who now have Internet e-mail access and more, and there are suddenly boatloads (big boats, at that) of people experiencing the Internet through e-mail for the first time.

This book was developed and written for those who want to use and understand Internet e-mail without going through some icky trial-and-error process that has them accidentally sending messages to Bill Gates, who will in turn revoke their software licenses for Windows, Word and everything else Microsoft.

What You'll Find in This Book

Fun. Parties. Celebrations. A perfect-bound Mardi Gras. Well, not quite. The topic of e-mail is, well, boring. When I told my friends and family (here we go with MCI again...) that my next book was going to be about Internet e-mail, they nodded (some just dozed off immediately), which certainly isn't the most effective form of communication over the phone. Sometimes I could get a really fake "Oh, that's something that there should be a book on...be sure to get me a copy." Right.

So instead of rambling on about protocols (huh?), eunuchs and terminal refrigerators, this book will get you up and running with your Internet e-mail software, and then show you what to do so you don't make too much of a fool of yourself. Not that you would or anything, but it *can* be awkward to accidentally send a secret-admirer message intended for your high-school sweetheart to the 5,000 readers of the rec.weasel.pet newsgroup—especially if one of the weasel-newsgroup readers is your spouse, who just so happens to have lunch with your high school sweetheart every other Wednesday.

Even more important than learning about Internet e-mail is enjoying learning about it, so I've tried to make this book more fun to read than a pop-up book. Actually, I wanted it to *be* a pop-up book, but the publisher said uh-uh. I took that as a no. In lieu of that (yes, yes, I had to look up "lieu" to spell it correctly), I've opted for "witty" references and examples, as well as the occasional pun.

You can read this book in order, or you can flip to the page that corresponds to the last two digits of last night's lotto number. After much consideration, I've dispensed with the encoded-password scheme that forced you to read the book in order, writing down key code words as you went along. So find a topic you want to know more about and start reading!

Requirements to Use This Book

If you don't have an Internet e-mail account, or even know what that is, don't worry. Different chapters within the book take all the guesswork and confusion away from setting up your account. Chapter 3 in particular describes the different Internet and commercial online services, while Appendix A lists those services and how to contact them.

As far as your system requirements go, almost any Windows, Mac or DOS system with a modem can be used to send and receive Internet e-mail. If you have a computer at your office or school, ask the system administrator there if your system can send Internet e-mail (at which time you'll probably get the typical "yes, your system can send and receive Internet e-mail" in that condescending tone that only system administrators seem to have mastered). You don't need any special hardware (like something called a "Super Internet E-Mail Decoder Algorithm Ring") to become one with the electronic community, and software is provided from your access provider (once again, see Chapter 3 and Appendix A).

The only thing I can think of that you might not have that would be useful when reading this book is a twisted sense of humor, and you can usually get those really cheap via mail order. (See what I mean?)

Test Your New-Found E-Mail Skills

You can reach me by e-mail at the following address:

Toulouse@aol.com

Feel free to tell me anything you'd like, but please do mention that you're doing this only because I asked you to in this particular book. I welcome all comments, both positive and negative, and I'm also interested in seeing any nifty smileys or signatures that you've come up with. (Both smileys and signatures are discussed in Chapter 8, "Acronyms, Smileys & Signatures.") I can't promise a detailed response, but I will try to read anything that isn't more than three pages long, and I'll attempt to send at least an acknowledgment to you if I can.

You can also find my occasional posts, most often in the rec.comics.misc, rec.juggling and rec.mac.games newsgroups. As far as being available for seminars, mall openings and bar mitzvahs, send me a note and I'll check my schedule.

Before You Start

Make sure your modem is on, get your fingers relaxed and poised over your keyboard, and then turn the page.

Oh, and if you have a spouse, you might want to send him or her off to the mall or something....

E-MAIL: ON-RAMP TO THE INTERNET

The Internet. It's obsessive. It's feared. It's cool. It's hot. Hip people have their Internet addresses printed on their business cards and stationery. Extremely hip people have voice mail messages like, "I'm much too busy to answer my phone, but if you send a message to CouchTater@sofa.org I'll be sure to get back to you." Way-hip people are never seen, just spoken to through the Internet, making their very physical existence questioned.

E-mail. It's your link to the electronic world. More specifically, it's the gateway to the Internet. The first part of getting onto the Internet, in fact, is to get an e-mail address. Once you have this, everything else falls into place like those 12,000 dominos your neighbor spent two weeks setting up in his basement before that fateful minor tremor. Your Internet e-mail address makes you a part of the largest electronic community that has ever existed, enabling you to converse with anyone else in the world who also has an Internet e-mail address.

It's all quite a bit to comprehend, so if you start feeling dizzy, avoid reading this book on tilt-a-whirl rides until you feel better.

In the Beginning...

Well, at least back before computers existed (ask your grandparents, kids), there was no such thing as e-mail. Instead, there was only the Postal Service, probably one of the best-run government agencies of all time.... The Postal Service would stop by your house, apartment or business every day, picking up outgoing mail and dropping off incoming mail. It was a nice system, but it was slow. To send a letter across the country could take from five to ten *working* days, so with postal holidays figured in (they average what, one a week?) you never knew *when* anything would arrive, just that it would be later than you should expect it. Sending letters through "snail mail," as e-mailers call it, also cost more than it should, since postal rates seemed to rise geometrically with inflation.

Then, in the 1980s, the almighty fax machine ruled. Now, instead of waiting weeks for letters and messages, we got them in mere minutes. Except when the line was busy, or the fax machine was out of paper, or the toner was out, or it was drying off (unplugged) because the intern had spilled coffee on it earlier that morning. Until a few years ago, fax paper was crinkly, curly, strangely shiny, and under the constant assumption that its mission in life was to resemble a tube, not a flat rectangle. All this came at a time when the world was hating paper anyway and was busy predicting a utopian, paperless society, which won't happen until we run out of trees (of course, by then we'll be growing genetically enhanced trees so we can make more paper from them...). But all that aside, fax machines—and their accompanying baggage—became a necessity.

In the background of these massive volumes of written communication was the computer revolution, which made computers part of our everyday lives. No longer did you need to take out a second mortgage and forgo Junior's college education to buy a computer system. Big, faceless corporations began buying more and more computers, and other faceless corporations rose up to build and sell them. Although they were everywhere, computers really had never been tapped for their true communications ability. Instead, word processing and desktop publishing generated even *more* paper, which needed to be sent to its readers through the Postal Service or fax.

The Internet Comes Alive

And you thought Peter Frampton was the only one.... The Internet first came into being during the '70s; a creation of the Defense Department, which designed a network of computers called ARPAnet. The new network, which was built to survive all sorts of natural and manmade disasters like earthquakes, nuclear war and Roseanne's marriages, consisted of several computers linked to one another through high-speed networks in a manner that allowed the network to continue running, even if one computer should cease to function properly. (A computer? Function improperly? Nah...)

Then, in the '80s, greedy little scientists (as opposed to the generous larger variety of the '90s) created a high-speed network called NSFNET (National Science Foundation NETwork), which replaced the aging, slower-than-molasses-on-a-cold-day-in-January-at-the-Arctic-Circle ARPAnet.

Eventually, companies started creating and selling gateway software and hardware that let private businesses and corporations connect to this network, and the Internet as we know it (well, I know it; you may not yet, but you will) sprouted to life.

The original NSFNET has been replaced with higher-speed lines since then, and another replacement of some type will probably occur again before the turn of the century. At the current rate of growth, the Internet should eclipse its current usage maximum within two years, at which time *something* is going to have to be done to increase its capacity.

So, Where Does E-Mail Fit In?

Because there are so many ways to access a system that is somehow connected to the Internet, almost everyone who has a computer and a modem can inexpensively become part of this "global network," as the media types like to call it. And once someone has become connected to the Internet, he or she has an e-mail address, which can be used to send and receive, of all things, Internet e-mail.

The more people, companies and organizations that gain access to Internet, the more valuable the Internet becomes. Once everybody in the world has Internet access (not that far-out of a concept, as Greg Brady might say), it will become totally indispensable.

Internet ≠ Computers

Many people equate computers and the Internet. This has got to be the most common misconception floating around outside of cyberspace today. Computers have very little impact on the Internet; they just provide the tools needed to access the Internet. The Internet is really made up of people from around the world, each of whom is a small part of the whole; without these people interacting, there would be no reason to *have* an Internet.

And the nice thing is, you hardly need to know anything about computers to send and receive e-mail. Some of the basics are helpful, but if you can write a letter to Grandma Myers in Microsoft Word, you already have more than enough computer knowledge to feel comfortable with this Internet e-mail stuff.

E-Mail: A Quick Definition

E-mail is short for electronic mail, which is mail that is created and sent electronically. More accurately, it is mail that is created and sent by a computer somewhere and received by a computer somewhere else. E-mail can contain most text characters, but has no special formatting options, so you may want to forget about using a font like Lefty Casual (one of my favorites) or *making* every *other* word *italic*.

You will run into two types of e-mail during the course of your Internet travels: Intrasystem e-mail and Internet e-mail. Intrasystem e-mail is e-mail that stays within a particular system, like your network of PCs at the office, or e-mail that the people who subscribe to commercial online services (like America Online and CompuServe) send to each other. Internet e-mail, the main focus of this book, is instead e-mail that can travel to anyone on *any* system, as long as that system is connected to the Internet.

For instance, Internet e-mail can be sent from a user of one online service to another, like the e-mail your friend Joe, who has a Prodigy account, sends to you on America Online about all sorts of things, not the least of which is his impatience with Prodigy's lackluster Internet support.

The @ Symbol

The @ symbol, called the "at" symbol, is the key to Internet addresses. When an electronic address has the @ within it, it means that it can receive mail from anywhere on the Internet. If the electronic address doesn't have an @, the person either forgot it or doesn't have a mail gateway connection to the Internet.

What's All This Talk About Gateways?

In order for a system to access the Internet, it needs to be connected somehow. If you aren't fortunate enough to have access to a computer that makes up one of the systems belonging to the Internet system, information you send and receive must go through a *gateway* to get to the Internet and back.

A gateway is simply a device that allows all the information on the Internet to be read by all the different systems out there. The best analogy I can think of is *Star Trek*'s Universal Translator. It's a device built into the communicators of Starfleet personnel that somehow (I don't know how—it's the 23rd century and everything) converts any language to something they can understand. Those same Universal Translators are built into the microphones so that when the shows are taped, the viewing audience doesn't need a translator to understand what that giant flowing goo-alien from Voltra-XII is saying.

Most commercial services access the Internet by using a gateway device of some sort. A technical definition of Internet gateways is beyond the scope of this book, mainly because they were created by engineers, most of whom don't speak an iota of English (not English that you or I could understand, anyway).

How to Get an E-Mail Address

There are three ways to get an e-mail address. These methods are listed below.

Free, Unlimited Internet Access

If you work for a company or college/university that has company-wide or college-wide access for its employees, you're in that small percentile of the truly blessed. You may be able to get totally and completely free access to the Internet, complete with an e-mail address. If you don't work for one of these fine institutions, and you plan on spending a lot of time on the Internet sending and receiving mail (as well as taking advantage of other Internet services), it may be time for a career change.

Usually the institution that provides the service will also provide software for a variety of Internet activities, including e-mail.

Internet E-Mail & More

Several commercial online services, such as America Online, Compu-Serve, Delphi, GEnie and Prodigy, provide Internet e-mail addresses as part of their package. These services will usually charge a fairly low monthly fee as well as hourly rates ranging from $2–$25 per hour, depending on the service, time of usage, and other options (they charge more for extras like stock market reports, up-to-the-minute sports scores, and passenger-side airbags).

In addition to varying Internet-related capabilities, each of these services offers its own unique combination of subscribers, message boards, software and events.

Usually, your sign-on name is the first part of your address (more on addresses in Chapter 2, "All About Internet Addresses"). Each Internet service provides online guidelines for all of its mail capabilities, which makes the learning curve fairly easy to navigate.

A complete listing of commercial services is found in Appendix A, "Internet E-Mail Services."

Internet Access at a Price

The most expensive way to get an Internet e-mail address is by hooking up with an Internet service provider. These companies provide several different levels of Internet support for business and individuals, offering more Internet capabilities than the commercial services listed above.

Depending on the type of service, you may be charged just a monthly fee or a monthly fee and a small hourly fee. There are two good reasons to get an e-mail account through an Internet service provider. First, it allows you to access, explore and send messages through the Internet at a faster pace than cheaper services. And second, it provides you with in-depth Internet capabilities that go far beyond the typical user's needs.

Some service providers will supply the software you need to connect to the Internet, or you can get shareware products from an online commercial service or from a local BBS (bulletin board system), which is sort of like a low-cost or free commercial service. There are also several different commercial products available from different companies for Mac, Windows and DOS platforms.

I have an account with an Internet service provider that charges me a monthly flat fee only, since I spend (waste, some would say) hours and hours reading and sending e-mail, looking through newsgroups, and engaging in other types of generally mindless Net surfing.

An extensive listing of Internet service providers is found in Appendix A, "Internet E-Mail Services."

Moving On

Now that you have some background on this e-mail stuff, we'll hurry right along into the area of electronic addresses. The seemingly indecipherable codes that say where messages are coming from and where they're going are *the* scariest and nastiest-looking part of Internet e-mail, or so says my friend FubieRob@aol.com.

If you just can't wait to get right into the sending and receiving of e-mail, skip ahead to Chapter 3, but don't tell anyone about it. I wouldn't want the people who read Chapter 2 to riot.

2

ALL ABOUT INTERNET ADDRESSES

Your electronic address is your identification when you send and receive Internet e-mail. Without an address, you couldn't really function at all—you'd be an Internet invalid. This chapter is all about what makes up Internet addresses and how to send Internet e-mail from one system (or service) to another.

What's in an Address?

Your electronic address consists of two parts: your user name and your domain. Your user name is usually the "name" you use to sign on to your Internet service, which on most systems is an 8- to 10-character word. A few systems are different, such as CompuServe, whose users sign on with an impersonal 9-digit number. My user name on America Online is Toulouse, a name I chose for several reasons (see sidebar).

Most online services allow you to pick your own user name, which can be anything you would like it to be. Some consideration should go into this decision, since you usually can't change your user name once you've chosen it. People often choose a name that is similar to parts of their own names, like SammyAdams or TRoosevelt. Other times they will choose something that reflects a hobby, skill or occupation, like IJuggle, LuvGoddess or MrMailMan. And then there are those who prefer to remain anonymous, like SAY7812 or IML84AD8.

Choosing a name can be difficult because that name or one very similar to it might already be in use on your online service system. For instance, since I have the screen name of Toulouse on America Online, no one else can have that name. Similar names may pop up with different spelling variations, like Toolouze or Too Loose, but Toulouse may not be duplicated. This assures that my electronic user name is unique to that system.

Master of Your Domain

This is all good and pleasant, but an e-mail address needs more than just a name—otherwise, dire consequences would result. Let's say someone on eWorld chose Toulouse as his or her user name (so we both had the same user name, but on different systems), and then someone else on the Internet sent a message to Toulouse. Both of us (America Online Toulouse and eWorld Toulouse) would get that message, even though it was intended for only one of us. To prevent this type of confusion, all Internet addresses include the domain of the user.

The domain is simply the place where you have your user account. That can be an online commercial service like Prodigy, CompuServe or

Toulouse Seems Like a Silly Name But there are some good reasons (at least I think so) why I chose it as part of my Internet e-mail address. First and most important, it's a unique name that isn't too hard to remember (not like JoeBob442 or Carla-Rama5). This is critical since many people I talk to communicate with me only through e-mail, and they don't want to be looking up my e-mail address every time they want to send me a message. Besides, as you'll see below, the story behind the name makes for great Internet e-mail fodder.

The name itself was chosen because Toulouse is the name of my cat, a handsome young fellow. He was named after Toulouse, one of the three kittens in Disney's animated 1970 film *The Aristocats*. The other kittens were Marie and Bérliose, their mother was Duchess, and Thomas O'Malley ("the alley cat") was Duchess's love interest. Toulouse's hobby was painting. My cat's hobbies are eating, sleeping and eating.

The best line in the film comes after Edgar, the motorcycle-riding evil butler who has kidnapped →

GEnie. It can be an Internet service provider, or it can be the company or educational institution where you work.

Each domain has its own domain "name." The domain name for CompuServe is compuserve.com. The domain name for Columbia University is columbia.edu. The domain name for America Online is aol.com.

@ Again

Remember that silly @ symbol we mentioned back in Chapter 1? The @ is pronounced "at" when it appears in an e-mail address. It is the link that goes between your user name and your domain name. The @ symbol tells your system that yes indeedy this mail needs to traverse the Internet looking for that particular user, since he or she doesn't reside within the same domain as the sender. Of course, if the recipient of the message does reside within the same domain, you don't need the @ symbol at all, or the domain name that follows it. For instance, a user with an America Online account could send mail to "Toulouse" and it would still get to me.

The Full Address

My complete address for my America Online account then, with all the bells and whistles attached, is Toulouse@aol.com, pronounced "Toulouse at a-o-l dot com." Toulouse is my user name, @ says that I can be reached through the Internet, and aol.com says that my account is on America Online.

(kittynapped?) Duchess and the kittens, is chased by two dogs off a road, at which time the basket with the cats is thrown from the sidecar of the motorcycle into a field. Duchess, Marie and Bérliose all start calling "Toulouse, Toulouse, where are you Toulouse," until a little brown head pops up from inside the basket and says, "Right here, Mama." Well, maybe you should go see it yourself if Disney ever re-releases it in theaters or if it finally makes its way to home video.

The Toulouse in the film was named after Henri de Toulouse-Lautrec, a French painter who is known almost as well for his public outrageousness and short stature as for the contemporary posters he painted around the turn of the century.

This whole turn of events works out very nicely, since I've always had an interest in art, and have written books on computer software used for creating digital artwork. Of course, I'm about 6'5", and I try not to be too socially outrageous. In addition, I've never been to the city of Toulouse, located in France, though my cat may need his own ZIP code soon.

My eWorld account is Toulouse@eworld.com, pronounced "Toulouse at eWorld dot com," and my CRL account is Toulouse@crl.com, pronounced "Toulouse at c-r-l dot com." Of course, the only reason this works for me is that Toulouse was available as a user name when I set up accounts at each of these services.

The corporate robotic non-human sentinels at CompuServe give you a number, which you can't change. How personal of them. My CompuServe account (which I'm not going to include, since my buddies there charge a per-message fee for sending and receiving Internet e-mail) is something like 19922.4321@compuserve.com, pronounced "one nine nine two two dot four three two one at CompuServe dot com." Even though my CompuServe account name (number, whatever) is something like 19922,4321 when I send mail within CompuServe, the comma is changed to a period when someone sends *me* Internet e-mail.

Commas, apostrophes and spaces aren't part of Internet e-mail addresses; commas and apostrophes are replaced by dots, and spaces are deleted.

Top-Level Domain

You might have noticed that all of my Internet e-mail addresses end with .com. The last set of letters is usually referred to as the top-level domain name. These letters represent the type of domain at which a user resides.

The .com in my addresses means that all the services I have an account with are commercial services. The chart below shows several of the most common top-level domain names and their "meanings."

A Word to the Devious   So you don't even try it, my eWorld account is also Toulouse. I also use Toulouse on any service that lets me use a name. It makes things easier that way, trust me.

"Dot," Not "Period"
A "." in the middle of an electronic address is always pronounced "dot." If you call it a period you run the risk of public humiliation and shunning. Well, you'll only be shunned if you're Amish, in which case you probably don't have a computer or an Internet connection, making the whole point about shunning moot. Even if you won't get shunned, avoid saying "period" when you see a "." anyway.

Some people don't say the last "." that appears in an Internet address. This has started to become common practice, so if someone says something like "a-o-l com," ask them if a dot should go in between the a-o-l and the com (it always goes there, but this gives you a chance to show your superior Internet know-how without offending anyone).

Domain Name	What the Name Means	Description
.com	Commercial	Businesses that provide Internet access and related services for a price. You can obtain a list of these services by sending e-mail to info.cix.org (a nonprofit organization, oddly enough—see below).
.edu	Educational	Usually reserved for universities, colleges and places of learning.
.gov	Government	These domain names indicate that the information sent from these addresses has been made available to the public.
.mil	Military	This is actually a bit more exciting (at least more exciting than government). Most of these addresses are restricted; the ones that aren't don't contain anything worth reading.
.net	Network Resource	Addresses that contain information on either (1) the Internet or (2) a local network.
.org	Organization	Any nonprofit organization that has a specific interest in almost any area, from the International Jugglers' Association to Beekeepers of America.

Over the Top

Occasionally you might spot an address like CarolA@racc.edu.uk. This address would indicate that it is an educational address in Great Britain (United Kingdom), hence the .uk at the end. Not all addresses in foreign countries have these little two-letter extensions to their domain names, but many do. See Appendix C for a fairly comprehensive list of countries and their domain extensions.

Even though it seems like a logical thing to do, do *not* include the country code in the domain unless it is specifically noted in the recipient's Internet e-mail address. Doing so will probably result in unsent e-mail. Along the same thought, don't add .us to your friend's address just because he lives in Toledo. E-mail addresses with the .us code are rare.

Don't Prove Me Wrong   All of you Internet dwellers with .us extensions: don't send me Internet e-mail just to show me that yes sirree you have a .us extension. I know you're out there, but you don't make up that significant a portion of the Internet population to warrant a mention other than "rare."

In contrast, I would have to say that non-.us Internet addresses should get a mention of "well-done," which by itself doesn't mean much and even as a play on words is stretching it quite a bit.

Sending Mail to & From Online Services

If you want to send mail to someone who uses a different system or service than yours, there are some important things to be aware of when sending e-mail across the Internet.

Most services have adopted (or will shortly) the common addressing scheme used in the Internet, such as Toulouse@aol.com, for both sending and receiving mail, but there may be some discrepancies. Below is a listing of the major commercial online services and their domain names, with an example of how mail could be sent to your pal Johnny "Dough Boy" Cellulite.

Service	Domain Name	E-Mail Address
America Online	aol.com	DoughBoy@aol.com
Applelink	applelink.apple.com	DoughBoy@applelink.apple.com
AT&T Mail	attmail.com	DoughBoy@attmail.com
CompuServe	compuserve.com	12345.5434@compuserve.com
Delphi	delphi.com	DoughBoy@delphi.com
eWorld	eworld.com	DoughBoy@eworld.com
GEnie	genie.geis.com	DoughBoy@genie.geis.com
MCI Mail	mcimail.com	DoughBoy@mcimail.com
Prodigy	prodigy.com	DoughBoy@prodigy.com

Getting mail to people at these services is the easy part. Some services make it a little more difficult to send mail out from their systems. Check with the commercial service provider to see what the requirements are for your service (I'd list them here, but they've been changing faster than I can dial their numbers to check 'em out).

Names on the Internet

Some user names change from the original system user name to their Internet name equivalents. No spaces or punctuation aside from periods can be used in an Internet address, so the following substitutions take place:

- Lucy Ann becomes LucyAnn
- Linus Tyrone O'Malley becomes LinusTyroneO.Malley
- 33224,9586 becomes 33224.9586

Finding Addresses

If you don't know your buddy Ralph's Internet e-mail address, and you want to drop him a note explaining in detail (okay, call it bragging) about your enormous and comprehensive understanding of the Internet, call him and ask him what his Internet e-mail address is. Sounds awfully anticlimactic, doesn't it? Until some new system is incorporated into the Internet, most addresses for individuals will not be readily available. There are ways to look for addresses (see below), but the effectiveness of most of them is questionable, especially compared to reaching out and grabbing someone by the ears via the phone system.

And then there is the possibility that Ralph doesn't even *have* an Internet e-mail address. Or that he shares his address with others that he works with. Or that he has asked his online service to keep his address confidential.

Once you've called Ralph and found out his Internet e-mail address, do the unthinkable and write it down somewhere, or at least stick it inside an electronic address book. It seems silly at the time, especially when Ralph's e-mail address is RalphyDude@delphi.com, but you'd be surprised how easy it is to forget that RalphyDude has a *y* in it and not *ie*, or that he is on Delphi and not eWorld, etc. I've taken to writing Internet e-mail addresses right on my Rolodex cards for that person, even if I have stored the address in my online address books.

The Plight of Multiple Internet Services   If you have more than one online service, you're asking for trouble, Internet e-mail-wise. Of the several accounts I have, I use two of them the most: my America Online account and my CRL account. Unfortunately, I send mail to other people from both of these services, as well as the other, lesser ones.

The problems begin when I send a message to someone from America Online with whom I have been regularly corresponding by using the CRL service. Looking back through old mail on AOL doesn't display any of the mail I've gotten from this person on CRL. To reference that mail, I've got to log off AOL and sign onto CRL, check the mail, and then either return to AOL or send from CRL (yikes!).

To avoid having to sign on and off, I'll print out the Internet e-mail that I think I'll need to reference in the future. Besides wasting paper, this habit results in a totally disorganized mess of correspondence.

The moral of the story? If you have more than one Internet e-mail address, use only one of them for correspondence, and don't tell others what your other addresses are.

To make things easier for your friends, and to avoid annoying phone calls like, "Uh, do you have an Internet address?" print your Internet e-mail address on your business cards. You can also include it in stationery, advertisements or anywhere else people look for addresses and phone numbers.

Next to the above-mentioned phone call, one of the easiest ways to find someone's Internet address is to look at the "From" line in any mail that he or she has sent you. The address will always be formatted perfectly, and you can copy and paste the address directly into your "To" line.

Another way to find addresses is to purchase one of the Internet white pages guides available. The drawback of this method is the considerable lag between the time the information is entered and the time the book appears on bookshelves (and even longer until you notice it on those bookshelves and plunk down the moola to buy it). For those individuals who pride themselves on stability, Internet e-mail addresses will be current. But for the vast majority of Internet explorers, change is the only constant. Between job changes, students graduating (and dropping out), and users switching over to "better" or "cheaper" service providers, few people retain the same Internet e-mail address longer than a couple of years.

Advanced Address Finding

There are a few ways to hunt down addresses using services available on the Internet. Each of them is discussed below.

If You *Know* This Person Has an Internet Address

It's important to know if someone even *has* an Internet address. If you aren't sure about this "minor detail," all the time spent searching might be in vain. The closest thing to a universal Internet e-mail address finder (sort of like a giant electronic address book for the Internet) is some-

thing called the knowbot, which is slowly gaining widespread acceptance. The knowbot is a program that searches for a name on various mail servers it has access to, then lists the Internet e-mail addresses that match your query. The most discouraging current limitation is that many online services (most of them, actually) don't yet have a method to allow the knowbot to search their address database. For instance, if your friend has an eWorld account, you won't be able to find his or her Internet
e-mail address through the knowbot, since eWorld currently doesn't make this information available to the knowbot.

To use the knowbot to search for Internet e-mail addresses, send the following e-mail to kis@cnri.reston.va.us. Leave the subject line blank, and in the body of the text type only the following:

> query *name*
> quit

Instead of the word "name," type in the name of the person whose address you are looking for. You may use first, last, or first and last names. Of course, if you used "Ted" as the name, there would be hundreds or maybe thousands of responses to your query.

After a short period of time (usually less than an hour in off-peak times), you will be sent a listing of the knowbot's attempts to find your name. The following message is a sample result mailing of a name query using the knowbot service, looking for "Toulouse."

```
To: toulouse@crl.com
Subject: kis results
Reply-To: kis@CNRI.Reston.VA.US
Status: RO
X-Status:


Welcome to the new KIS mail server at CNRI.


kis input >> query toulouse


Connected to KIS server (V1.0).
Copyright CNRI 1990. All Rights Reserved.


Trying whois at ds.internic.net...


The ds.internic.net whois server is being queried:
_____

Garth, Danielle (DB403)          Garth@LAAS.LAAS.FR
    CNRS-LAAS
    902 av du Colonel ROCHE
    31077 Toulouse Cedex
    FR
    +33 61 33 6424


    Record last updated on 04-Jul-90.
_____

Taylor, Pierre (PC137)          Taylor@TLS-CS.CERT.FR
    ONERA CERT
    10 Avenue Edouard Belin
    BP 4025
    31055 Toulouse Cedex
    FR
    +33 61 55 70 47


    Record last updated on 04-Dec-90.
_____
```
→

```
Walsh, Patrick (PL102)          Walsh@IRIT.IRIT.FR
    IRIT
    Universite Paul Sabatier
    021 Route de Narbonne
    31062 Toulouse Cedex
    FR
    +33 61 55 63 03

    Record last updated on 04-Dec-90.
    _____
Doherty, Daniel (DG318)              DTY@CWI.NL
    Laboratoire d'Aerologie
    012, route de Narbonne
    F-31062 Toulouse CEDEX
    FR
    +33 61 55 69 49

    Record last updated on 21-Jan-93.
    _____
Priestly, Daniel (DN64)   Priestly@ZEUS.UNIV-POITIERS.FR
    Institut National des Sciences Appliquees de Toulouse
    209 Avenue du Recteur Pineau
    86022 Poitiers CEDEX
    France
    FR
    +33 49 45 39 82

    Record last updated on 23-Feb-93.


The nic.ddn.mil whois server is being queried:

No match for "TOULOUSE".

Trying mcimail at cnri.reston.va.us...
Multiple matches found, results may be incomplete.
```

```
Name:           Franklin Toulouse
Organization: UNUM
City:           Portland
State:          ME
Country:        US
E-Mail:         490-9021@mcimail.com
Source:         mcimail
Ident:          490-9021
Last Updated: unknown

Name:           Franklin W. Toulouse
Organization: UNUM
City:           Portland
State:          ME
Country:        US
E-Mail:         610-0120@mcimail.com
Source:         mcimail
Ident:          610-9021
Last Updated: unknown

Trying ripe at whois.ripeput >> quit
```

In this example, most of my results were from Internet addresses whose users live (or work) in Toulouse, France. Only one person was found in the U.S. with the name Toulouse.

The result can often be disappointing, since the knowbot can access only a small percentage of systems connected to the Internet. This situation is sure to improve, though, and eventually most, if not all, systems will make their address databases available to the knowbot.

If This Person Has Posted to Usenet Newsgroups

If you know that the person you are looking for is active in the Usenet newsgroups (see Chapter 9), you can find his or her address simply by sending the following message to mail-server@rtfm.mit.edu (again, leave the subject line blank):

> send usenet-addresses/*name*
> quit

Once again, using both the first and last name for your search will bring the best results.

Yo, Postal Dude!

If you know someone uses a particular service—like your cousin Lezley, who has an America Online account—you can send a message to the postmaster for that service, asking him or her to forward a message to the recipient.

"But," you ask, "if I don't know the person's user name, how can I tell the postmaster to forward it to him or her?" Darn good question. The thing is, you tell the postmaster that the name of the person is Lezley Gehman, and then the all-powerful postmaster looks up the name on the service's user list. Once the postmaster finds Lezley's user name, he or she can forward the message to her. If there are several Lezley Gehmans (like if she has been cloned or something), the postmaster may send the message to all of them, hoping the correct one will respond to you, or send you a message saying that there are too many, and you need to be more specific. Some will actually provide you with a list of screen names to choose from.

A good message to send would be this (of course, if you don't have a cousin named Lezley who has an America Online account, you may want to change some of the details):

Lies, Lies, Lies   The addresses of users sprinkled around this book are altered so that these people won't have to receive unnecessary e-mail from all the readers of this book. As a general rule, it is poor etiquette to publish anyone's e-mail address. My addresses throughout this book are good ('cept the CompuServe one), though, so you can e-mail me till you're blue in the face (of course, I probably won't read it or respond...).

```
To: postmaster@aol.com
Subject: Forgot your e-mail address...

O Great and Powerful Postmaster Sir, I've mis-
placed my cousin's Internet e-mail address. Her
name is Lezley Gehman, and she has an account with
your online service. Thank you.

Lezley,

  Hi there, it's Ted. I forgot your Internet e-
mail address, and am having this message forwarded
to you. Could you please reply with your Internet
e-mail address?
  By the way, how's that hardly working husband of
yours doing? Ha ha ha. I'm kidding, at least as
far as you know. Ask him the Bugs Bunny phrase for
me...
  Relatively Yours,

Ted
```

Remember, the postmaster is doing you (and your recipient) a favor, so be polite and humble when requesting a forward like this. The postmaster will usually strip out the message to him or her before forwarding the message to its intended recipient.

Intrasystem Address Finding

Many commercial services provide some method of finding other users of the same service that you use. On large services, such as America Online and CompuServe, you may find a large number of individuals with the name you are looking for. Once the major services make their user addresses available to the knowbot on the Internet, finding addresses will become much easier.

Check with your commercial service to find out what types of address-finding services it provides.

Moving On

Now that I've addressed this address issue, you can address the next chapter, which addresses not addresses, but instead addresses where to put addresses when addressing e-mail, in addition to addressing non-addressing issues.

3

SENDING & RECEIVING INTERNET E-MAIL

Like going up against the American Gladiators Zap and Power, the basic functions of Internet e-mail can be rather frustrating and intimidating, making you wonder if this whole computer messaging business is worth its weight in sand. This chapter provides a quick look at some of the software that's out there for Internet e-mail, as well as some of the different aspects you might not have considered before.

Unlike *American Gladiators*, there's quite a bit more to Internet e-mail than appears on the surface, as you'll read below.

E-Mail Software & Consistency

There are countless methods of sending Internet e-mail through different software packages. Some e-mail programs are stand-alones, like Eudora, while others are part of an online service software package, like the mail-sending capabilities of America Online. Then there are other mail programs that are part of a UNIX system, like Elm and Pine.

All of these Internet e-mail programs look different, but most of them work very similarly. In fact, once you take out the intrasystem capabilities of the Internet e-mail software, they're pretty much the same. Shown below is a sample mail window from America Online, one of the easiest and most functional Internet e-mail software packages.

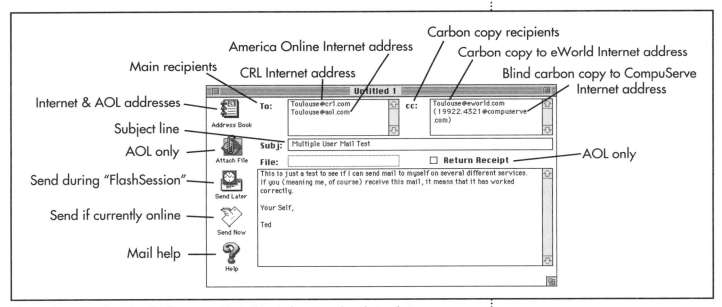

Figure 3-1: *The America Online e-mail interface is functional and simple to use.*

The functions labeled in the figure are described throughout this chapter. Note: Two features of the America Online mail system, Attach File (files that accompany the message) and Return Receipt (a notification sent to you when the recipient reads the message), are not available on certain Internet e-mail systems. Check with your service provider.

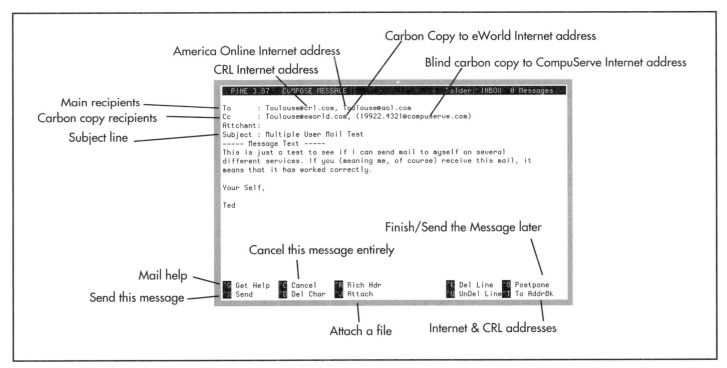

America Online Internet address
Carbon Copy to eWorld Internet address
CRL Internet address
Blind carbon copy to CompuServe Internet address

Main recipients
Carbon copy recipients
Subject line

```
 PINE 3.87   COMPOSE MESSAGE                   Folder: INBOX  0 Messages

To      : Toulouse@crl.com, Toulouse@aol.com
Cc      : Toulouse@eworld.com, (19922.4321@compuserve.com)
Attchmnt:
Subject : Multiple User Mail Test
----- Message Text -----
This is just a test to see if I can send mail to myself on several
different services. If you (meaning me, of course) receive this mail, it
means that it has worked correctly.

Your Self,

Ted




                                               Finish/Send the Message later

              Cancel this message entirely

^G Get Help  ^C Cancel    ^R Rich Hdr       ^K Del Line   ^O Postpone
^X Send      ^D Del Char  ^J Attach         ^U UnDel Line ^T To AddrBk
```

Mail help
Send this message

Attach a file
Internet & CRL addresses

Figure 3-2: *This Pine e-mail software interface is a little less intuitive, but it's just as functional.*

Another type of Internet e-mail software is found in a UNIX shell system. Above is an example of the same message shown in the previous figure, but done using the Pine mail software.

If you are a Macintosh or Windows user, this nasty-looking interface can be quite intimidating. If it doesn't bother you, it is just as functional as the America Online software, and even more so in some ways.

I won't bother showing an example for each of the available Internet e-mail software packages—there are just too many of them. Instead, you'll find that the capabilities and features discussed throughout this chapter can be applied to almost all the Internet e-mail software that's out there, floating in the ether(net) of the computer world. Of course, depending on your Internet connection, you might not have a choice about which software to use, either.

E-Mail Message Parts

The main parts of any e-mail message are the address line (usually "To"), the carbon copy line (usually "Cc"), the subject line and the message. The only part that absolutely *has* to be filled out is the address line, though some e-mail systems will require something in the subject line.

Address Line

This line contains the Internet address of the person you are sending mail to. As described in Chapter 2, "All About Internet Addresses," it should be in the format *username@domain.topdomain*. If you were sending a message to Toulouse on America Online, this line would read as follows:

> To: Toulouse@aol.com

If you want to send this message to more than one recipient on the Internet, place a comma between each of the addresses you wish to use. The number of addressees you can list on your address line will vary according to which software program you use. If I wanted to send Internet e-mail to three of my friends, each on different services, my address line would look something like this:

> To: Fletcher2@comix.com,87778.1220@compuserve.com,
>   Jfilbert@eworld.com

Analogy Misfire   I wanted to include tips on how to stay on that platform in Joust, and my pattern for climbing the Wall, but my publisher said that all this *American Gladiators* stuff really didn't fit the topic that well. He also mentioned that the entire *American Gladiators*/Internet e-mail analogy was just plain silly, so I e-mailed him a challenge to race me on the Eliminator. He responded with a wry comment involving all sorts of things like deadlines, royalties and his incredible sentiment for the unemployed who sit around watching low-rated syndicated television shows.

And I thought Lace fought dirty...

If it makes you feel better (and neater), you can insert spaces after the comma, since Internet mail routers will ignore the space anyway.

Carbon Copy Line

The Cc line mystifies many a new Internet e-mailer. What is it? Chocolate cupcakes? Candy corn? Coke can? (You can see where my thoughts lie...) Depending on who you ask, it is either the carbon copy line or the courtesy copy line. Either term is fine, though carbon copy is the more accepted of the two forms. Some Net dwellers will tell you that Cc *has* to be courtesy copy because you don't use carbon paper with Internet e-mail. Of course, these are the same people who have tan lines from their computer monitor.

You can use the carbon copy line if you want someone—other than the person you've sent the message to—to read that message. Why would anyone want to do this? Let's say you've gotten a personalized Internet e-mail letter from Stephen Hawking, arguably the greatest scientific mind alive today (next to some of the guests on *Rikki Lake*). You send him a reply, and also send a carbon copy to your tenth-grade physics teacher, who gave you a "D," just to show him that maybe your equations were right, and that if he has a problem with that he should remember that you correspond with Mr. Hawking. In no time your physics teacher will be appearing on "Teachers Who Cheated Their Students and Now Pay for it by Receiving Spiteful E-Mail Carbon Copies," the topic of the day on *Rikki Lake*.

You fill out the carbon copy line in the same way as the To line. You can also send multiple carbon copies by typing in several addresses, separating them with commas. The lines below show the message being sent to three friends and carbon copied to two others.

> To: Fletcher2@comix.com,87778,1220@compuserve.com,
>   JFilbert@eworld.com
> Cc: Pandora@crl.com, Prudence3A@genie.geis.com

Blind Carbon Copies

No, this isn't about how to Braille-encode your message. A blind carbon copy is a secret copy of the Internet e-mail message you are sending, so that no one but the blind carbon copy recipient knows he or she is getting the message.

Of course, your Internet e-mail message window may not provide a Bcc line (I've never run across one, anyway). If that's the case, then to blind carbon copy someone, put that person's address in parentheses, and then place the whole shebang in the Cc field. Some e-mail services will allow you to put blind carbon copies in the To field, but check to see that this works before you try it and all your girlfriends find out each other's e-mail adresses because your system *doesn't* support this method. Our example continues, this time with one blind carbon copy going to Tallulah (hey, my friends were born in the '60s, it's not *their* fault).

Who's It From? It may surprise you to learn that there is no "from" line to fill out when you send an e-mail message. Miraculously, Internet e-mail systems automatically include the sender's information when a message is sent.

This is yet another example of computer efficiency shaving, what, three seconds off the time it takes to send a message. Just think, after sending 600 Internet e-mail messages, you'll have saved enough time to watch one of the lost episodes of *Dobie Gillis.*

> To: Fletcher2@comix.com,87778,1220@compuserve.com,
> JFilbert@eworld.com
> Cc: Pandora@crl.com, Prudence3A@genie.geis.com,
> (Tallulah@davidson.edu)

In this example, nobody but Tallulah would know that Tallulah is getting this message.

In general, blind carbon copies are frowned upon on the Internet. There aren't too many good reasons to use this feature, so avoid it unless absolutely necessary. Some Internet e-mail systems will not allow you to send blind carbon copies, in which case you must send either a regular carbon copy or a forward of the entire message to the recipient.

Subject Line

The subject line is a line of text that describes the subject of the message. It is proper etiquette to be as descriptive as possible when filling out the subject line (see Chapter 7, "E-Mail Netiquette Primer," for the do's, don'ts and donuts on Internetiquette), so that readers with tons of mail know if they need to look at your message immediately, if at all.

"That sounds rude! Why wouldn't they want to read my message?" you ask, and for good reason. Understand, though, that because Internet e-mail messages find their way to all sorts of people, recipients often receive more Internet e-mail than they have time to reply to.

I get an average of 25 messages a day, many of them from people I've never heard from before. I don't have time to read and reply to most of my Internet e-mail, so I scan the subject lines for topics that either (1) interest me, (2) praise something I've written, or (3) trash something I've written. Subject lines like "Hi" and "I wanted to know..." might get passed over until I have time to sort through my Internet e-mail, which happens about once a week.

I know many people who receive so much Internet e-mail that they *never* read unsolicited messages unless the subject line makes it imperative that they do.

Of course, if you're sending mail to your mom or your spouse, it's not quite as essential to make the subject line sound important. You would hope that these people would read the message regardless of what the subject line says. On the other hand, if you're a mom sending messages to your kids, you'd

Mail Troubles, Part I   Y'ever have one of those days? Of course you have; especially if your work involves computers in any way. Sometimes things just won't go as planned when you're creating and sending Internet e-mail.

For example, let's say you need information from a mail server or another site (see Chapter 9) that requires you to leave the subject and/or message portion of your Internet e-mail blank in order to process your request. Unfortunately, though, you are working on a system that won't send your mail unless you have *entered something in one or both of these areas.* What do you do? This Catch-22 can really wreck an otherwise productive computing session, "forcing" you to quit for the day, and to change your focus to exploring the island of MYST (hey, I've been using this "computer's got me down, gonna play a game" thing for years, and my wife *still* buys it).

To get around this obstacle, enter a space in the subject line and/or the message field. Most mail servers and other sites that require blank subject or message fields don't pay any attention to spaces, and will read the line as being blank.

be better off putting dollar signs and other enticements in your subject line in order to get the ungrateful little brats to read the message. "Mom's sending me 50 bucks? I'll e-mail her a thank you."

The Message

This is undoubtedly the most important part of your Internet e-mail. For a complete rundown on how to structure the contents of an Internet e-mail message, see Chapter 5, "Understanding E-Mail as a Medium."

Most Internet e-mail systems can send mail of any reasonable length (several pages). If you run out of room, you can always break your Internet e-mail message into two pieces and send two messages instead of one. If you do so, make sure the subject line of each message states that yes indeed there are two parts to the message, and that it notes which part is included in each e-mail message.

The Internet can send only standard ASCII characters, so things like bold and italic characters, as well as bullets and ellipses, probably won't make it through very well. Instead, they might look like M*^H^ü11^D^ or something that makes even less sense. I use the see-it use-it keyboard rule, which goes something like this:

If I can see the character on a key on my keyboard, it can be used in Internet e-mail.

Follow this rule and you'll never have to worry about your e-mail turning into something that resembles an assembly-language program (if you don't know what that looks like, you're already one of the blessed few).

Mail Troubles, Part II Using a "bad" address can cause more major e-mail trouble. A "bad" address is one that (1) doesn't exist or (2) is in the wrong format. In either case, your mail is returned to you with all sorts of computerese UNIX gobbledygook that really means that your address didn't work. I had a problem recently when I tried to send my Christmas list off to the big guy. I didn't have the right address, so I got the following mail returned to me:

———

To: toulouse@crl.com
Cc: Postmaster
Subject: Returned mail: Host unknown
——— Unsent message follows ———
Date: Sat, 10 Sep 1994 19:56:17 -0700 (PDT)
From: Ted Alspach <toulouse>
Subject: My Christmas list
To: SantaClaus@North.Pole

Dear Santa:

   This year, I'd really like a few things, which I've listed below for your convenience. It goes without saying that I've been EXTREMELY good, especially if you don't count that incident with the State Trooper, so don't waste your time looking on that list of yours.   →

Okay, here is my list:

- Pentium 66Mhz PC w/ CD-ROM, 1.2gb hard drive, 21-inch Sony Trinitron monitor, 16-bit SoundBlaster card, Windows, MS Office, Tie Fighter, and a grab bag of some of the other games out there.
- Lexus, loaded. You pick the color, as long as it's red.
- PowerMac 8100/100 w/ CD-ROM, 2.6gb hard drive, two 21-inch Sony Trinitron monitors (I do a lot of DTP work), and bunches of Mac games.
- 11x17 PostScript printer, 600 dpi. Use your judgment to find me a good name brand.
- Tonka front-end loader to replace the one Dad ran over with the Chevy when I was eight.

Thanks, Santa, and if you have any questions, e-mail me back.
Your buddy,
Ted

To fix an addressing problem, you'll need to find the correct address (or check for typos—that's what always happens to old finger-mumbles here), enter it in the address line, and re-send your message.

If anyone knows the correct address for Mr. Claus, let me know.

Of course, if you have a Kanji keyboard (Kanji is a Japanese character set) you just happen to be that classic exception that proves the rule above, as well as a classic chump for being taken by the local Computer-Shop-N-Go minimum-wage salesman, who got you to buy a keyboard with Japanese characters.

Sending & Receiving Internet E-Mail

When you've finished creating a new message, your only task is to send it out to the person(s) you've addressed it to. You can usually do this by pressing a button or a simple key command. Receiving e-mail is even more mindless, as you'll see below.

Sending Mail

Like watching an *American Gladiators* interview segment ("So, Donna, what was going through your mind as Jazz was beating the tar out of you?"), sending Internet e-mail is almost a mindless activity. Find the Send command or button on your message screen, and activate it. You may get a prompt asking if you really want to send your e-mail, in which case you press or click Yes (or OK, on some systems). After that the Internet e-mail will disappear from your screen, starting its long journey across the Internet toward whatever grand destinations you've sent it to.

Receiving Mail

The only thing you have to do to receive e-mail is to make sure the sender has your e-mail address. The mail will appear in your e-mail program, at which time you should click the Read button or select the Read command. The mail will appear, as shown below. Figure 3-3 shows mail sent from the CRL location to America Online. Figure 3-4 shows how that same mail was received by the CRL service using the Pine e-mail software.

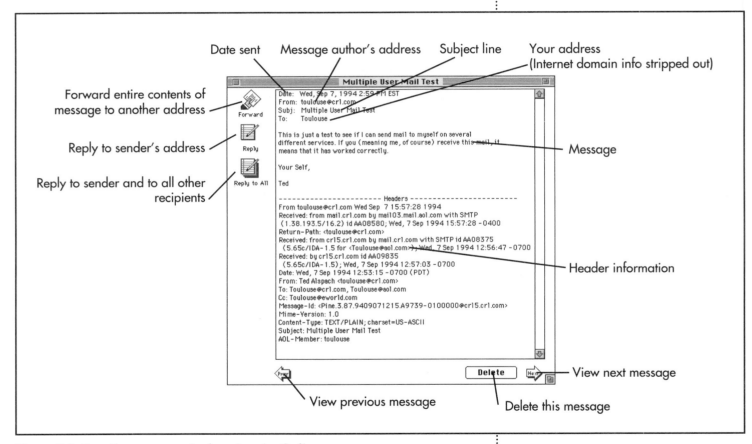

Figure 3-3: *E-mail message received on America Online.*

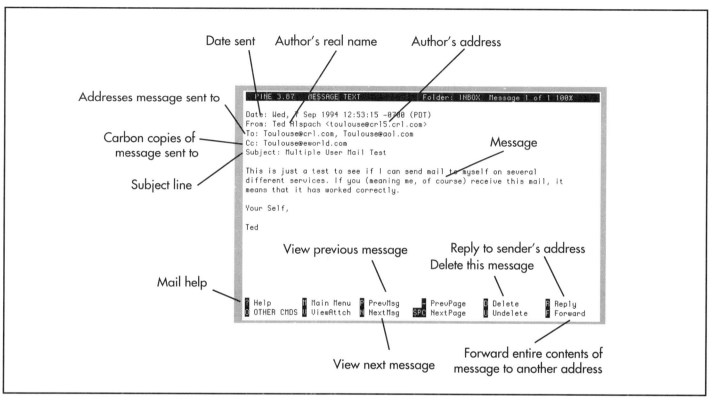

Date sent   Author's real name   Author's address

Addresses message sent to

Carbon copies of message sent to

Subject line

```
PINE 3.87   MESSAGE TEXT           Folder: INBOX  Message 1 of 1 100%

Date: Wed, 7 Sep 1994 12:53:15 -0700 (PDT)
From: Ted Alspach <toulouse@crl5.crl.com>
To: Toulouse@crl.com, Toulouse@aol.com
Cc: Toulouse@eworld.com
Subject: Multiple User Mail Test

This is just a test to see if I can send mail to myself on several
different services. If you (meaning me, of course) receive this mail, it
means that it has worked correctly.

Your Self,

Ted
```

Message

View previous message

Reply to sender's address
Delete this message

Mail help

```
? Help        M Main Menu   P PrevMsg    - PrevPage    D Delete     R Reply
O OTHER CMDS  V ViewAttch   N NextMsg   SPC NextPage   U Undelete   F Forward
```

View next message

Forward entire contents of message to another address

Figure 3-4: *E-mail received on the CRL service.*

Whenever you receive Internet e-mail, you'll see a really nasty portion at the top or bottom of the Internet e-mail message, called the header. These several lines of UNIXese describe the process the mail went through before it got to your mailbox. This information is not all that relevant for the average (even the above-average) Internet e-mail user. Some software, like Pine, removes the header info for you (see Figure 3-4).

The top of the Internet e-mail message will contain the date and time the message was sent, the address of the message's author, the subject line and the message's recipient(s).

Other Internet E-Mail Options

Now that you have this Internet e-mail message in front of you, there are a number of things you can do with it. The most common options are explained in the sections below.

Delete

If you've read your Internet e-mail, all the while muttering "yah-dee yah-dee yah-dee," you might want to get rid of the message. You also might want to get help for that muttering problem. You do this (getting rid of the message, not getting help for muttering) by deleting the message. If you don't delete your Internet e-mail, it sits around in your mailbox, and either pops up every time you enter your mail program, or lurks in your service provider's system, taking up valued hard-drive space.

Deleting mail is usually as simple as pressing a Delete button or selecting a Delete command. Many mail programs will ask you if you are sure you want to delete the mail, at which time you should click the Yes option, not go into a lengthy diatribe about how of course you want the mail deleted or you wouldn't have pressed the Delete button, and so on.

Once you have deleted your Internet e-mail message, it is gone for good. Be sure you want to do this when you select the Delete option, or you'll end up with a darn good reason to spend the rest of the afternoon blowing away the baddies in Doom II.

Reply

Replying to an Internet e-mail message allows you to return a note to the sender without having to fill in the address and subject lines. This of course shaves yet another three seconds off the average message sending time, providing you with enough time every 600 messages to catch the entire "E-Mailing Men Who Hate Women and the Women Who Love Them Enough To Reply Back" Maury Povich show. The address automatically becomes that of the original sender, and the subject becomes Re: *Original Subject*, where the original subject is the subject line of the original message. (For example, if the subject line of the original message reads "You should be writing me a huge check," the same line on your reply will read "Re: You should be writing me a huge check.") The "Re" stands for *reference*, not reply.

After that, your reply is pretty much like an original mail message, so you can pretty much enter anything that strikes your fancy. You may want to copy portions of the original message in your reply so that the recipient knows what the heck it is you're rambling about now. When you do quote someone, it is proper format to indicate copied portions of messages by marking them in one of the two ways shown in the figures below. In these figures, I am replying to the message sent throughout this chapter.

Figure 3-5 shows what is probably the most common quoting method. Quoted text is indicated by > at the left edge of each line. Certain Internet e-mail software may already do this for you when you choose the reply option. Figure 3-6 shows an easier method for quoting text, using double >> (sometimes >>>) at the beginning and end (<<) of each section of quoted text.

And This Little Piggy Went Re:Re:Re:Re: All the Way Home   No, I don't have a speech impediment (besides, I'm typing, which would be another type of impediment altogether). When replying to a reply, your Internet e-mail software will most likely stick another re: onto the front of the message, which already has an re: sticking out of it. This can re:sult in re:peating re:'s, re:inforcing this re:minder: re:member to re:fuse to use more than one re: in a subject line, or you'll re:gret it.

It's proper to get rid of any re:'s besides the original. A better thing to do instead of using multiple re:'s is to put a number at the end of the subject line in parentheses that tells which re: this is. So our subject line of this chapter would look like this after four cross-replies:

Re: Multiple User Mail Test (4)

Now, this works best if the person you are sending the message to adds to this number, instead of Re:re:ing, or just deleting their re:.

```
>This is just a test to see if I can send mail to
>myself on several different services. If you
>(meaning me, of course) receive this mail, it
>means that it has worked correctly.
>
>Your Self,
>
>Ted

Ted:
I found this message to be annoying and a loud,
preposterous interruption of my otherwise quiet
and peaceful afternoon.

My Self,

Ted
```

Figure 3-5: *The most common e-mail quoting convention.*

```
>>This is just a test to see if I can send mail to
myself on several different services. If you
(meaning me, of course) receive this mail, it
means that it has worked correctly.

Your Self,

Ted<<

Ted:
I found this message to be annoying and a loud,
preposterous interruption of my otherwise quiet
and peaceful afternoon.

My Self,

Ted
```

Figure 3-6: *A somewhat easier way to indicate quoted text.*

Forward

Forwarding your Internet e-mail is useful when you want someone else to read messages you've received, along with any of your comments. For instance, I sent much of my work on this book to an America On-line address for my publisher, Ventana Press. If the recipient (my editor) gets my Internet e-mail and thinks to herself, "Gee, what the heck is Ted talking about now? I wish my Latin interpreter could take a look at this...," she could forward my Internet e-mail message to her Latin interpreter, at ig.pay.@in.lay.

To forward a message, click the Forward button or select the Forward command. You can then type a message (as you would for a reply), which will accompany your forwarded message. The recipient will receive one file, with your original message at the top and the forwarded message at the bottom.

View Next/Previous Message

Most Internet e-mail software allows you to go to the next message—or back to the previous one—by either clicking a button or pressing a command key. This action doesn't delete the Internet e-mail message you were viewing—it just moves you along to the next (or previous) one.

Saving Messages

Most Internet e-mail software packages have a save feature that allows you to save your Internet e-mail for future reference. If you don't save your Internet e-mail, it will usually sit in an area of your "mailbox" for about 30 days or until your mailbox has too many other newer messages. Then it is automatically deleted. The length of time and amount of Internet e-mail you can keep there vary with different systems.

The messages you save are copied to your hard drive (or to your service provider's service area), where they remain until they are deleted. A good rule of thumb is to save only those messages you are *sure* you will need in the future, and let the rest sit in your in-box until they disappear. If a message has been sitting in my in-box for 30 days, I don't care if the system does delete it automatically. On the other hand, if I've just used material from mail in my in-box, I might save it at that point so that it won't disappear.

Moving On

Hey, if you've read straight through to this point, congratulations! No more icky nasty technical "click-here-and-press-this" chapters in the rest of the book. From now on everything is practical, interesting and fun. And no more *American Gladiators* references. I promise.

In the next chapter, I'll tell you if your mail is safe from prying eyes (it's not) and what you can do about it (not all that much). Read the chapter anyway.

4

E-MAIL SECURITY & PRIVACY

According to current consensus, the active mega-conspiracy theorists—the ones who are certain that not only do Hitler's clones (all three of them) and two of the supposedly deceased Kennedy brothers hold meetings at Graceland that will shape future human genetic evolution, but that radiation poisoning has been and will continue to be present in certain brands of microwave popcorn—are the ones behind the big conspiracies.

You know, the whole Jackson/Presley thing, the hidden truth that Reagan *was* killed by an assassin's bullet and immediately replaced by a prototype advanced Disney animatronics robot for the next seven years of his (its?) presidency, and that one man is behind the scenes at both Coke and Pepsi, pulling the strings and reaping the profits. Those are the *big* ones.

Of course, these are grand conspiracies that no one talks about in public. There is another conspiracy-in-the-making that *is* public, one that will have a tremendous impact on our electronic and eventually our everyday lives. This is something that is being propagated by our government so that it has the ability to read our Internet e-mail as well as invade our electronic privacy in other ways. More on this in the section entitled "Clipper Chip: Uncle Sam's Secret Decoder Ring," later in this chapter.

When you write a letter to your Aunt Spam in Cleveland, do you think anyone will read it but your aunt and maybe Cousin Fredo? When you send Internet e-mail to someone, it's like sending a letter across the country...without an envelope.

Pass the Word, Please

The world is obsessed with security, and for good reason. Without locks on our doors, we are making ourselves prime targets for thieves, burglars, murderers and disgruntled postal workers.

How many passwords do you have? I have more than 10. Passwords for my ATM card, credit cards, online accounts, certain software programs, files that I've encrypted.

Without passwords guarding our electronic information, we make ourselves prime targets for *crackers*, known originally back in the '80s as hackers. Crackers are people who, for money or thrills, spend a good deal of time trying to get to that information that you have guarded so carefully with passwords.

Password Selection

Some online services will allow you to select your own password. One of my online services said the pass-

Cracker Conspiracy, Part I Your access to your online service requires a password. It is the only way that you can sign on, read your Internet e-mail, and do any of the other things that can be done online. Without this password, you're out of luck...or are you? What happens when *you* forget your password? You aren't locked out permanently, are you? No, you call your online service and act really sheepish and tell them that you've forgotten your password. You don't even have a clue as to what it could've been. They verify your identity and give you your password.

So what happens when a *cracker* (a guy, let's say) calls your online service and pretends that he's you? He acts really sheepish and says that he's forgotten *your* password. And what if he's lifted a credit report on you and can provide the necessary information asked by the online service attendant? Looks like you're suddenly sharing your account.

I'm no cracker, but as research for this book, a friend of mine ("Ritz") tried to get my password for one of my online services, just to see if it could be done. He didn't have all the information needed, but he could've gotten it if he tried. Of course, trying to get someone's online-account password is breaking the law, as is using that password.

word I initially chose wasn't complex enough, so they added to it! If you are in a position to select a password for your account, keep the following rules in mind:

Don't write it down anywhere. This sounds like Passwords 101, but if a person wants to get into your account and then finds your account written down, you've handed him or her the key without a struggle. If you absolutely have to write it down, use some type of encoding that only you'll understand—like using every third character and writing it backwards. And then hide that paper. Or just don't write it down in the first place.

Don't tell it to anyone. You are the only person who will ever need your password. If someone asks for it, don't divulge it. If the person persists, tell him or her something that definitely *isn't* your password. Report any password requests to your system administrator immediately, giving the user ID of the individual who asked for it.

Don't pick an "easy guesser." What's an easy guesser? A friend, pet or family member name; a date, especially a birthday of yourself or someone close to you; anything involving your Social Security number; phone numbers; celebrities or popular media characters; words that are found in an abridged dictionary.

Combine numerals and letters. If you use only numbers in an eight-character password, there are 10 million combinations. It seems like a lot, but 10 million is nothing to a cracker's code-breaking program. Using a combination of letters and numbers ups the number of possible combinations to 2,821,100,990,000, which we can safely round off to *3 trillion* combinations. That should about do it.

Make your password easy to remember, but hard to guess. Of course, this sounds much easier than it is, and it doesn't really sound that easy. If someone you know could guess your password before someone you don't know could guess it, your password is too easy to guess. If you have to write it down, it's too hard to remember.

Who Can Read Your Internet E-Mail?

Legally, no one can read your Internet e-mail. But the individuals who run your Internet access system have the means, if necessary, to read your e-mail. In fact, since Internet e-mail is sent along from computer to computer on its way to its final destination, anyone at one of those systems could snatch up the mail going through and read it.

As far as I know, this never happens. If it did, and someone were caught, it would change the way most people send e-mail across the Internet.

Preventing Prying Eyes From Prying

The best way to secure your mail from any intrusions, including someone who knows your password, is to use an encryption program to encode the message of your text. Mac, Windows and UNIX platforms all offer several encryption programs, but the catch is that the recipient must also have a copy of the encryption software to decode the message.

A better solution is software called PGP, for Pretty Good Privacy (really—I'm not making this up). PGP is becoming the standard encoder that encodes plain text of messages, and can be decoded by anyone else with PGP. Here's how it works. If you are a PGP user, you have a private key and a public key. The private key only you know. The public key is the password others can use to encrypt a document if they want to send you private messages. That public key can be decrypted only by your private key. You can give your public key to anyone might be sending you messages in the future. The unique thing about this system is that you don't have to give the decrypting password to anyone,

Cracker Conspiracy, Part II What do you suppose an online service system administrator or tech person is paid? In contrast, how much money do you think that person could get for selling passwords of all the users in his or her system? Having this information for big commercial online services would be worth literally millions of dollars. Seems awfully tempting, doesn't it?

And what if an aspiring cracker were actually to land a job as a system administrator for one of these online services? He/she would have access to everything, and would have a pension building all the while.

Do online services make their employees take the same types of psychological profile tests that new FBI and CIA recruits take? Somehow I don't think so.

just the public key, which can't be used to decrypt the message. PGP is available on many Internet FTP (File Transfer Protocol) sites, and offers a version for most platforms.

Clipper Chip: Uncle Sam's Secret Decoder Ring

The Clinton administration has approved the use of something called the Clipper Chip, a device that will ensure perfectly encrypted messages with schemes that can't be broken, except by the U.S. government.

Of course, even if you trust the government not to pry (right), what about the CIA undercover operatives who quit or whom the government failed to "silence," who have access to the technology that allows them in through the Clipper Chip's back door? If you've seen movies like *Under Siege* or *In the Line of Fire*, you know that these operatives exist in fiction already....

Keeping Your Identity Anonymous

If you are the secretive type, you can send Internet e-mail to someone without revealing who you are. There are a few different ways to do this, but the easiest one is to send your mail through an *anonymous remailer*. After it receives your message, the anonymous remailer will strip out all of your information from your header and forward the message, using a code name in the From field.

The standard format for anonymous remailing is located at anon@anon.penet.fi. Before you send any anonymous messages, you need to choose a password by sending the following message to password@anon.penet.fi, keeping the subject line blank:

    Sniggle34poo18A

This would set your password to Sniggle34poo18A. You will need this password to send anonymous mail in the future, so make this password something memorable but different from your sign-on password for your online service.

Once your password has been set, you can send messages as follows, placing the subject in the subject line and the message text after the first two lines:

To: anon@anon.penet.fi
Subject: My First Anonymous Message

X-Anon-To: Tallulah@davidson.edu
X-Anon-Password: Sniggle34poo18A
This is my first anonymous message. I hope you have no idea who this is sending it to you...

—A secret admirer... :*

The X-Anon-To line tells the remailer where to send your message, and the X-Anon-Password line tells the remailer what your password is.

After you send your first message, you will get a response informing you of the "code" name that will appear on the From line of all messages you send. After that, all messages you send through this service are "anonymous." No one can use the knowbot or a Whois command to discover the code name identity.

If you wish to pick your own "code" name, send Internet e-mail to nick@anon.penet.fi with the nickname you want in the subject line. If you have further questions, send e-mail to help@anon.penet.fi.

Another benefit (sort of) of using anonymous remailers is that all replies you receive are also automatically "coded," so that you don't know who is replying. Of course, common sense should tell you that it is the recipient of your original message.

In addition, anonymous remailers provide a double-blind way to take part in a mailing list, so if you want to participate in one that you

Cracker Conspiracy, Part III   So, despite your best efforts, a cracker has found out what your password is for your online service. I doubt he'll stop there. No, he'll definitely try that password on your ATM account, credit cards and everything else you've ever safeguarded with a password.

Who can remember 10 passwords? Of course you can't, so you use the same one for your VISA as your Internet provider. Your ATM code and your long distance PIN are also the same.

You can very easily be at the mercy of someone you've never met.

find a little embarrassing (like goatees.r.great), don't worry; no one on the mailing list can track you down and find out your identity.

The Great Virus Scares: Safe Computing

Computer viruses have pretty much faded from the news recently, thanks to widespread use of anti-viral software. There are still all sorts of computer viruses lurking about, though, and a wise Internet user will take the necessary precautions when downloading files via the Internet.

Viruses are portions of computer code that are designed to (1) replicate themselves and (2) screw up something. Viruses don't exist in text files per se, but instead in any file that isn't plain text, like programs, resource files, extensions and the like. E-mail that doesn't have an attached file can't have a virus (at least not at this time).

If you do get files that are prone to viruses (see Chapter 9, "Mailing Lists, Newsgroups & Files"), be sure to scan them with anti-viral software *before* using them.

Net Schemers & Dreamers

There are as many unscrupulous individuals skulking around the Internet society as you'll find in the real world—maybe even more. There are several hoaxes and money-making schemes out there, as well as individuals who see the Internet as yet another place to sell goods.

I'd advise you to ask a fellow Internet dweller about something before you do anything rash, like sending money, continuing a chain letter or sending a postcard to a boy dying of cancer in England. Most of these are pointless schemes; some of them designed to make money, others not.

If you ever receive Internet e-mail with "Make.Money.Fast" in the subject line, do yourself a favor and don't read it, just delete it immediately. It is a four-year-old electronic chain letter. If you send this message to anyone else, you will be regarded as the lowest of lowlifes on the Internet, and you'll be flamed (see Chapter 7, "E-Mail Netiquette Primer," for more about flaming and getting flamed) rigorously.

Moving On

Of course, this whole issue of security is pretty irrelevant if you don't use your Internet e-mail service provider for anything more than to send mail to your aunts and uncles, keeping them up on your life, what's been happening...hey, that's really nobody else's business, is it?

In the next chapter, we'll begin to look at the real substance of Internet e-mail. We'll examine the advantages and disadvantages of Internet e-mail as a means of communication, and we'll compare it to other forms of communication, including personal contact, the telephone and the good ol' U.S. Postal Service.

5

UNDERSTANDING
E-MAIL AS A MEDIUM

What, a medium as opposed to a petite or an extra large? But seriously, it's important to place Internet e-mail in its proper perspective among the many different methods of communication available. As a contemporary form of communication, e-mail is unique. In fact, you'd have to go back an awfully long way to find its most similar forerunner—the telegraph. You probably weren't around when it was in use, but if someone needed to send a message quickly, the telegraph was the way to go. The message to be sent could consist only of words, which were transmitted from one telegraph station to another. The telegraph operator near the recipient would decode the message as it came in and have it delivered to you personally, if that was possible.

Although Internet e-mail is in some regards an offshoot of older forms of communication, it has abilities and features that transcend any medium the world has ever seen or used, a fact that makes many new Internet e-mail users squirm with obvious discomfort, like the way people react after they've shaken hands and then heard you say how glad you are to be just about through with that nasty bout of typhoid fever.

This chapter will give you the down-and-dirty information about how and when to use Internet e-mail as opposed to sending a letter by snail mail (you remember the U.S. Postal Service, right?), overnighting a letter, making a phone call, sending a fax or chasing someone down for a personal confrontation like something you'd see on a typical episode of *Melrose Place*.

Right Smack Dab in the Middle

The following chart shows different characteristics of the most common communication media in use during the mid-'90s.

Medium	Time to Arrival	Status	Response Intimidation
Personal contact	Instant	Above average	No escape
Phone call	1 minute	Medium	Extremely high
E-mail	1–10 minutes	Above average	High
Fax	1–5 minutes	Medium	Above average
Overnight delivery	1 day	High	Fair
Letter sent through the Postal Service	2–6 working days	Below average	Very low

The *medium* is the method used to convey the message. The *time to arrival* is how long it takes for the message to reach its destination. (The time it takes for someone to actually read the message can vary tremendously.) The *status* of the medium is how important or impressive it seems. The *response intimidation* is how much that medium demands a reply or response.

As you can see from the chart, personal contact is by far the most effective form of communication; it happens instantly and demands a response (unless the recipient has a penchant for running down the street, away from anyone approaching). By contrast, a letter sent through the postal system can take a long time to arrive, and once it has, it is easy to ignore. The recipient doesn't even have to open the envelope—he or she can just throw everything away, without even looking at the letter inside.

E-mail fits snugly in the center of all of these. It arrives fairly quickly and provides a high amount of intimidation for a response. The biggest drawback to sending e-mail is that the recipient's system may not be online when your message comes in, in which case the person will have no idea that there is mail sitting in his or her mailbox, patiently waiting to be opened.

The status of e-mail varies according to the recipient. When I get an overnight package from FedEx, I open it right away. When I get e-mail, I might let it sit a little bit before reading it if the subject line doesn't require my immediate attention. This probably isn't the case for everyone, and it definitely wasn't always the case for me; when I received very little e-mail, I read everything right away, regardless of the author.

As Internet e-mail becomes a more standard form of communication—and as users get "used" to using Internet e-mail for everyday correspondence—its status will diminish.

E-Mail as an Alternative

When is it proper to use e-mail instead of other, more traditional communication tools? This can be extremely difficult to recognize. (Of course if your recipient is not on the Internet, it is extremely *easy* to recognize.) One way you can make this choice is to compare the advantages and disadvantages of Internet e-mail with those of the other forms of communication. Keep in mind that Internet e-mail is most definitely not a replacement for other communication options, but instead yet another alternative in the media grab bag of the '90s.

Personal Contact vs. E-Mail

If contacting someone in person is the most effective form of communication, it is also the most difficult. First of all, it entails going out and finding the person you want to contact, which can be highly inconvenient and impractical.

In addition, the messages you exchange through personal contact are almost completely spontaneous. Unless you've memorized a script, the words that come out of your mouth may not be exactly what you mean, or what you want the recipient to hear. Finally, being confronted face-to-face can put the recipient on his or her guard, which can make all communication extremely difficult.

Internet e-mail is a much easier communication option. To begin with, it's extremely convenient, and it doesn't require business attire. In fact, if you have a laptop computer, you can be sitting in your hammock wearing boxer shorts and a tiara (I have walls around my yard so the neighbors don't think I'm weird) while sending a message to the president of a giant corporation. In addition, you can take all the time you want to create an e-mail message that contains all the information you want to convey. Of course your eloquent, alliterative and well-organized message may never stir up a response—the recipient can just blow off your messages with the delete command without ever reading them—but it is more likely that your message will be received and responded to.

Phone Calls vs. E-Mail

The phone is a much more convenient form of communication than personal contact, simply because you don't have to go anywhere or leave your comfortable perch to make a phone call (we have phones in our bathrooms, just in case). Of course all this convenience business may be kind of a waste if your recipient doesn't want to talk to you and is an expert at ducking calls. The good news, though, is that there are sleazy, underhanded ways to get around those situations (see sidebar).

Another advantage to using the phone is that it gives you an upper hand over your recipient. First of all, there is the element of surprise. You know you'll be speaking to the recipient, and can plan accordingly. You can even refer to written notes during your conversation, because you have had the opportunity to organize your thoughts and write them down. Your recipient, on the other hand, will often have no idea who is on the phone when he or she picks it up. Then there is the issue of control. As the caller, the direction your conversation takes—at least initially—is up to you.

Sending Internet e-mail temporarily provides you with the upper hand, because it gives you an opportunity and a forum to express your thoughts and agenda. In addition, you can make sure that everything you want to communicate is written, whereas in a phone

Calling Deception   Getting through to a recipient who would rather soak in hot oil than talk to you takes quickness, brains and chutzpah. Some people are blessed with all three.

Take Dick Pease, a former client at the company where I work. Dick owed the company quite a bit of money—he had several outstanding invoices—but that didn't stop him from calling when he needed technical support. One time when he called our salesman answered the phone, and Dick asked for me. The salesman thought he recognized Dick's voice, and started stalling him with all the common small talk salespeople learn in their "Small Talk 101: Breaking the Ice" course in sales school (which is a prerequisite to "Boring Clients To Death 126: What To Do If They Really Die On You"). Dick then proceeded to lie and say he was someone else, and the salesman passed along the call to me. Of course, when I said "Hi, Dick," the salesman, standing outside my door, was rather miffed, but Dick had done the job and gotten through.

conversation there is constant interaction, including questions and interruptions by the other party.

Unfortunately, you lose some of that power after you send your message, because you aren't forcing an immediate response. The recipient can take his or her time to examine your message thoroughly, and to formulate a reply.

Faxing vs. E-Mail

The form of communication most similar to e-mail is the fax, although there are some distinct differences between the two. First of all, the majority of fax machines currently use thermal paper, which curls and has kind of a dry and slimy texture. For that reason, the printing on a faxed message is usually hard to read and often illegible—unless the fax is sent by a fax/modem attached to a computer. The quality of Internet e-mail, on the other hand, is always as good as that of the text that appears on the recipient's computer monitor.

When you fax something you have to deal with several annoyances: you have to print out your message, send it through the fax machine and then throw out the paper, saving the original on a computer (if you're using a computer to create your faxes). Of course, the big advantage to faxing is that you can send anything that appears on paper to anyone else who has a fax machine. This is true of Internet e-mail too—that is, you can send a message to anyone with an e-mail address—but since more people currently have access to fax machines than to e-mail, the advantage for faxing is greater.

Overnight Delivery vs. E-Mail

Overnight delivery is an extremely expensive method of communication, but it is the one that gets the most notice. Nothing perks me up as much as the Airborne Express truck stopping at my house for a delivery, except maybe the FedEx van.

On the other hand, I'm also quite delighted to see several messages waiting for me when I sign on with my Internet e-mail service provider. Obviously a big drawback of e-mail compared to overnight delivery services is that you can send only a message, not a package.

One of the advantages e-mail has over overnight delivery from the sender's point of view is that it's much easier to type the recipient's e-mail address than to fill out the 1040-like overnight airbills.

Postal Service vs. E-Mail

The thing that everyone hates the most about the mail is the time it takes to get to your mailbox. Running a close second is the fact that each day at least one bill is present in the slush pile. And of course, junk mail appears. Sending mail through the Postal Service is equally frustrating.

E-mail beats up on conventional mail in the time department. It also cuts down on the pack-rat syndrome (unless you print out all your e-mail), characterized by the sheer inability to throw out that letter from Aunt Matilda, especially since you think you're in her will.

E-Mail: A Weapon of Death?

The good news about e-mail is that it is probably the easiest form of mass communication. As long as you know the recipient's Internet e-mail address, you can send him or her a message in just a few seconds. You don't have to get up, you can be eating potato chips, you can be naked at your computer (not advisable in an office setting unless you're desperate for a date).

The bad news about e-mail is that it can be deadly. Why all the danger? Well, for starters there's the speed element. If your online service charges you on an hourly basis, and you are composing e-mail while online, you are less likely to take the time to read exactly what you've written, resulting in not just unacceptable spelling and grammatical errors (see Chapter 6, "E-Mail & the Decline of Grammar") but also a tone that actually seems rushed. If you have the capability to compose mail off-line, do so, because you can take your time to both write and review your e-mail before sending it. America Online offers this option to its subscribers, along with something called a "FlashSession," which automatically signs on, sends your composed mail, receives your incoming mail and signs off, dramatically reducing the amount of time you spend online.

Of course, if your tone does seem "rushed," it is a good alternative to other tones, like nasty, demanding or critical. All of these tones can be reflected in writing, regardless of how much we write, and are especially likely to occur when we're writing quickly, which tends to happen when composing e-mail. To avoid potential misunderstandings from quick e-mails, follow this rule:

Read what you've written at least once when you are finished writing.

This will prevent all sorts of potential problems that you could run into otherwise. Reading over what you've typed will allow you to remove all sorts of words that can impart a subliminally negative tone to your message.

Always read the entire message—from beginning to end—before making any corrections. Doing so will allow you to slip into the recipient's electronic shoes for a second and view your message from his or her perspective. Unless the message is several pages long, you should be able to remember the sentences you want to correct until after you've finished reviewing the entire thing.

Moving On

In the next chapter, I'll be telling you all sorts of things that you've forgotten since high school English class. I've forgotten much of what ol' Mr. Boltz taught me, but I've forced myself to learn it again for you, the readers, to benefit.

I promise there won't be vocabulary tests, pop quizzes or anything about prepositional phrases, but we could all use a quick review of the basics now and then. And in order to get your e-mail messages across in the clearest and most effective way possible, you'll want to pay attention to the same elements of good grammar that you'd use in any other form of written communication.

6

E-MAIL & THE DECLINE OF GRAMMAR

We ain't talking just the casual misuse of an adverbial or a misplaced modifier here but a total lack of grammatical respect for english (what, no cap?) inasmuch that all sorts of atrocities and defamation of culture (like the occasional multi-part speeches from Yakko, Wakko and Dot) take place within each and every little single message that is sent across the webbed wires of the Internet from user to user and back to yet another user in defiance of the laws of our language regarding nouns and verbs and almost every other kind of word that can be typed as well as punctuation as fast as an e-mailer's fingers can dance across their keyboard and which eventually culminates in several terribly hard to follow and cliché-ridden run-on sentences. Whew.

Spending long periods of time on the Internet definitely won't help your grammatical skills. Just ask my editors. *Ed. Note: No need to ask; we heartily agree that Ted's grammar could be improved tenfold. Twentyfold, even.*

Would You Send a One-Sentence Letter?

No, undoubtedly you wouldn't. Why, then, does it seem perfectly natural to send an e-mail message that reads in its entirety, "I just received the materials and after looking at them I'm impressed enough to ask for more"?

Normally, a letter containing the same information would be spread out over several paragraphs. It would begin with an introductory paragraph, and would then provide a few paragraphs detailing the arrival of those materials and what aspects were found to be impressive. Another paragraph to ask for additional materials would follow, and the letter would conclude with a paragraph thanking the sender.

But because e-mail has an urgent sense to it, messages sent through the Internet usually contain as little language as possible. In the process of crafting a message free of excess words, however, the e-mail writer often ends up tossing many basic rules of grammar out the window, like that whole noun/verb business.

Not Exactly a Bunch of English Majors There's an old joke about the Internet (well, it's not *that* old, considering the relative youth of the Internet) that goes like this:

Question: "If 10 million monkeys sat down at 10 million computers and started typing, what would you have?"

Answer: "The Internet"

If you don't get this, you're (1) new to the Internet or (2) such a part of the communication breakdown there that you try to add smileys to everyday speech.

Spelling Bees

One of the grammatical areas e-mail users overlook the most is spelling. I'm not talking about just acronyms (see Chapter 8, "Acronyms, Smileys & Signatures," for more about these fun little letter combinations), but common, everyday spelling errors. If you're typing along at a breakneck pace (or more accurately, a breakfinger pace) and you happen to type "hte" instead of "the," you might not notice it.

Your reader, however, will. Obvious spelling errors have about as much chance of being ignored as Rita and Runt have of finding a permanent home. And an "hte" instead of a "the" is about as subtle as a giant billboard. A reader who doesn't know you may assume that any-

Frequently Misspelled Words Here's a little list of some of the most commonly misspelled words.

absence	appropriate
acceptable	argument
accessible	aspirin
accidentally	asterisk
accommodate	authentic
accumulate	auxiliary
accuracy	bargain
accustomed	believe
achievable	beneficial
acquiesce	benign
acquire	biased
addendum	blatant
admittance	bologna
advantage	bulletin
aggravate	bureau
agreeing	calendar
aisle	caliber
amateur	cannot
analysis	captain
Animaniacs	carriage
anomaly	cerebral
anonymous	certain
answer	changeable
apparatus	coincidence
appearance	committee
appetite	competition

one flippant enough not to correct a blatant misspelling is probably careless, rushed, hurried and a mediocre typist at best. Most of these things are negative...not attributes you'd like to exploit if at all possible.

Words with switched characters stand out like a glass of sherry in a sports bar, but even worse are spelling errors that show you don't know the proper spelling of a certain word. If "undoutably" constantly shows up in your e-mail messages, many of your mail recipients will "undoubtedly" lower their opinion of you.

Another spelling area to watch for is the use of homonyms, which are words that sound similar but have different meanings. Probably the most common such error is the incorrect use of "to" vs. "too." Use "to" as a preposition (as in "this is the way *to* grandma's"), and "too" to mean "also" (as in "count me in, too") or "excessively" as in ("I'm too sick to travel"). And, of course, never forget the age-old rule, "I before E, except after C, unless it looks really really wrong." Or something like that.

No matter how good your spelling is, a spell checker is invaluable. If your e-mail software doesn't have a spell checker (most don't), you might consider composing your mail on a word processor that does, and then copying and pasting the text into a mail document. There are also software packages available (Thunder 7 is one) that check your spelling as you type, no matter which program you're in.

Put a Cap on It

Make sure that proper nouns and the first word in every sentence are always capitalized. Names like Pesto, Bobby and Squit should *always* be capitalized. Places like Anvilania should always be capitalized.

Be Punctual

Look down at your keyboard. See those two keys to the right of the "M" key? The first one is a comma, and the second one is a period. They are your friends.

E-mail messages are supposed to be fairly brief, but many messages always seem to be made up of overly long sentences that tend to ramble on and on without proper punctuation like this one resembling something that Yakko would say when cornered into going back into the water tower. Here's a basic rule of thumb when typing:

A sentence is too long if you need to stop for a bathroom break in the middle of typing it.

Here's an elementary list of when to use commas while writing e-mail:

- Use a comma to separate an introductory phrase or clause from the rest of the sentence.

- Use commas to separate items in a list (when there are more than two items).

- Use commas to separate multiple adjectives that describe the same noun.

- Use a comma when the pause it creates will make the sentence easier to understand.

Use periods to end sentences and to follow abbreviations like St., Dr., Mr. or Ave. Never put two periods next to each other. Three periods in a row form an *ellipsis*, which tells the reader that there is either more that wasn't written or that he or she should make up the ending to the sentence.

Semicolons (;) are used to join two independent thoughts in a sentence. Use semicolons sparingly; you can often use a period instead.

Colons (:) in grammar are not that delicate piece of anatomy that Slappy always complains to Skippy about, but instead are used to indicate the beginning of a list, a quote or a statement. Considering that colons are also used by computer systems to determine locations of files, you might be better off avoiding them in e-mail altogether.

concede	eccentric
conceive	ecstasy
conscience	efficient
conscious	elaborately
consistent	elicit
correspondence	eligible
courageous	eminent
courteous	endeavor
creditor	entirely
curiosity	entrepreneur
curious	environment
curriculum	epitome
decadence	erroneous
deceive	esoteric
decision	especially
definitely	etiquette
dependable	euphemism
depreciate	evidently
descend	exaggerate
description	except
desperate	existence
despicable	existential
deterrent	exonerate
dilemma	exorbitant
disappoint	explanation
disastrous	exponential
discernible	facsimile
discipline	familiar
distinct	fascinate
Dot	February

finesse	indestructible
flammable	inferred
fluorescent	initial
foreign	innuendo
foreword	instantaneous
forfeit	interest
freight	interfere
fulfill	irrelevant
gauge	irresistible
government	jeopardize
governor	judgment
grammar	khaki
grievance	knowledge
grieve	laboratory
guarantee	larynx
height	leery
heir	liaison
hemorrhage	library
hiatus	license
hierarchy	liqueur
hindrance	magazine
homogeneous	mayonnaise
humorous	mediocre
hydraulic	memorandum
hypocrisy	mileage
icicle	miniature
idiosyncrasy	miscellaneous
illicit	misspell
immense	moccasin
incident	mortgage

Use two hyphens together to create a dash. Even if your software can create en dashes and em dashes, chances are your recipient *can't* read them, and will instead get some strange gobbledygook of foreign-looking characters instead. Em dashes are used to offset a thought within a sentence, while en dashes are used in typesetting for minus signs and other times when a hyphen is too short.

While we're on the subject, don't bother hyphenating your e-mail to break up words near the right end of the line. What looks like a good place to hyphenate to you might end up in the middle of a line on someone else's mail reader, as shown below.

Your hyphenation:

> I've decided that there is no need to erad-
> icate all hyphens from Randy Beaman's prose.

What the recipient sees:

> I've decided that there is no need to erad-icate all hyphens from Randy Beaman's prose.

Parentheses are overused by a variety of writers, including the esteemed author of this book (naw...). Yes, even I have succumbed to overuse of parentheses on occasion (like Christmas, July 4th, etc.). Parentheses draw so much attention to themselves that instead of giving additional information about the phrase preceding them, they sometimes serve as a focus for the sentence. I've found that parentheses are best used to add or explain humor when the reader might not understand the funniness (it's a word, really) of the sentence.

Following are some other miscellaneous punctuation notes:

- Don't use a character that you need to press the Option or Alt key to see. Your readers most likely won't be able to read it. Instead, they'll see something like [x^r%%12@$q9], which probably means very little to them.

- Use ampersands (&) when possible, but only in lists of two items.
- Use the number sign (#, also called the pound sign) only to precede a number, like #3.
- Don't use [brackets] or {braces} in place of parentheses.
- Use a forward slash to separate "and/or" or "him/her" when appropriate.
- Don't use bullets (like the ones in this list). Instead, just use an asterisk (*).
- Don't use "curly quotes" like the ones shown here. Always use "straight quotes" in e-mail.
- Don't overuse exclamation points! It can become really annoying! Quickly!
- When making a statement that you are unsure about, follow it with !?
- Don't use a backslash (\) in place of a normal slash (/).
- Use asterisks or underlines on each side of a word or words you wish to emphasize, like *wacky* _excrutiatingly funny_ terms. I personally prefer asterisks to underlines.

Structure

Like all types of writing, e-mail messages require sound sentence, paragraph and document structure. Instead of forcing you to relearn what you slept through in Mr. Boltz's English class, I'll just urge you to remember the following:

- Sentences contain a single point.
- Paragraphs contain sentences that contribute to a single thought.

muscle	possess
naive	pursuit
necessity	queue
neighbor	recede
neither	receive
ninth	recommend
noticeable	remembrance
notoriety	resuscitate
occasion	rhyme
occurred	rhythm
offense	ridiculous
official	Runt
omission	sandwich
omit	scarcest
opinion	scene
optimism	scissors
pageant	seize
pamphlet	separate
paradise	sergeant
parallel	sincerely
paralysis	spaghetti
paralyze	Squit
participate	statute
pastime	succeed
peculiar	surprise
perpendicular	sustenance
Pesto	symmetrical
plateau	synonym
pleasant	temperament
pneumonia	temperature

The Brain	vague
till	variant
tragedy	veil
typical	veterinarian
unique	villain
until	Wakko
usage	weird
usually	wield
utilize	Yakko
vacancy	yield
vacuum	zealous

- An e-mail document should never be so long that it covers several unrelated ideas. Send separate messages for different subjects. This allows your recipient to focus on one message subject at a time, and respond instantly to those messages that require a simple answer, without sifting through excess information.

This last rule is easier to forget than you may think. The easiest way to make sure you stick to it is to write the subject line of your message first, and then to check back on it as you are writing. If the subject line is "Why I memorized the Animaniacs theme song," you better not stray off into discussing the square footage of that house you just bought. Send a separate note for that topic.

E-mail should fit onto a single 8 1/2- x 11-inch sheet of paper when printed. That limits you to a maximum of about 700 words (depending on type size, font, etc.). I *hate* to have to staple parts of my e-mail together when I print them out. There are very few instances when e-mail should be longer than one page. This should occur only when the subject matter calls for it.

Everybody's So Tense...

Try to use a single tense (past, present, or future) for your entire message, rather than switching from one to another. If you shuffled around until you are sitting in front of your computer until you will get up next week, readers are going to be confused. That last sentence moved from past to present to future, separated by "until." You have to read something like that a few times, and even *then* it doesn't make too much sense.

Ask yourself the following:

- *Did the subject do this already?* For instance, if Mindy has already escaped from Button's watchful eye, use the past tense.

- *Is the subject doing this now?* If Buttons is currently climbing a skyscraper construction project to follow Mindy, use the present tense.

- *Will the subject be doing this in the future?* If Buttons will follow Mindy down a girder around a sharp corner, lose his footing, and then plunge 30 stories into a giant vat of concrete, use the future tense.

Moving On

With the dreaded grammar chapter finally behind us, we can take a look at the behavior appropriate for e-mailing on the Internet—things you may do, and things you shouldn't do. Remember, the online community is as different as another country (say, for instance, Anvilania) in its rules of courtesy and etiquette. Just like burping is polite in some foreign countries (as well as in men's dorm rooms and anywhere when football is on television), there are many strange social intricacies to conquering the online world.

If you *do* plan on taking over the world, you should be pondering what I'm pondering: Improve your grammar, and leave Pinky in the lab.

7

E-MAIL NETIQUETTE PRIMER

Netiquette is not about what you should do when sending Internet e-mail, but rather about what you *shouldn't* do. There are all sorts of written and unwritten codes of behavior that as a citizen of the Net, you are expected to follow. Failing to follow these procedures results in either flaming, destruction of your credibility or both.

Opinionated Flame: Seriously, who asked you for your purely academic (and ultimately worthless) opinion?

Back to New Yawk

Let's say you live in New York City. More than any other place on this earth, in NYC you are expected to follow certain practices. If you get even a smidgen out of line the residents there will know you're a tourist. It's even tougher to fit in there than in a foreign country, for reasons that I have yet to discern.

One of the most important rules in New York is to avoid eye contact. If you're caught looking at someone you'll learn quickly not to do it again. Maybe you'll get a rude comment—"Whattaya lookin' at, freak?" Or, if you're really lucky, you'll receive a free shove along with the same remark.

Another important thing to do in New York is to refrain from looking upward, especially in Manhattan. Lifelong residents have seen enough skyscrapers to last them a lifetime. They know the buildings are there, so why bother looking up? Besides, it can make you dizzy.

People who live in New York take these things and many more for granted, and most of them assume that their behavior isn't just specific to a certain area but is a general rule of thumb everywhere.

Newbie or Not Newbie

If you are an Internet dweller (someone who spends more time in front of a computer terminal than sleeping), the rules and behavior concerning the Internet seem quite natural to you. So when another dweller does something wrong, it sticks out like a raw, festering sore.

Get a Life Flame: Even I don't spend every second sitting on my skinny butt and typing on my computer!

Some of this behavior "code" is pretty darn silly, but over the past 10 years or so it has evolved into an accepted set of guidelines. Those who violate that code are considered to be "newbies" (individuals who are new to Internet practices and etiquette—Internet "tourists"), regardless of how long they've been on the Internet. Newbies get little respect overall, and if you do a newbie-like thing, you'll be considered a newbie for a long time to come.

Lurk Before You Leap

You'll be in pretty good shape if you follow the guidelines in this chapter, but also be sure to spend time "hanging out" on the Internet—reading mail, newsgroups, Web sites, etc.—before sending anyone mail. The longer you lurk, as the practice of reading without writing is called, the less chance you'll have of making a newbie-like error.

You don't need to lurk forever; just lurk long enough to get a feel for the area of the Internet you're exploring. The most important thing to do when lurking is to look for FAQs (Frequently Asked Questions), compendiums of information that a newbie would typically ask on a certain subject. FAQs are maintained and updated by good-hearted souls who usually want nothing more than to not be bothered by the same questions again and again. And again.

What're You Scared Of?

Aside from being regarded as a newbie, you could also incur the wrath of old-time Internet dwellers (Internet users who have been Netting more than three months). The penalty? Flames. Just typing that word sends shivers up my spine.

Spelling Flame: Nice spelling. But then, at least you can impress the ladies by typing with your toes, huh?

A flame is a derogatory piece of e-mail (or a post in a newsgroup) that tears an individual apart. The most common recipients of flames are those Internet users who don't follow the Laws of Netiquette. Many flames are well worded, Don Rickles-style insults that poke fun first at the offender's intelligence, and second at his or her Internet knowledge. Some flamers will use profanity to clarify their point of view, while others stoop to juvenile cracks about the offender's mother, etc.

While a single flame is enough to send you into a bout of depression, hundreds of flames might just force you to change your e-mail address.

Realistically speaking, you need to do something *really* wrong or get the "wrong" person mad at you in order to receive boatloads of flames. Typical newbie mistakes *won't* get you this type of uncontrolled response, though I wouldn't want to risk it.

Accepted Rules of Conduct

There is no one particular place you can go to find the rules of Netiquette on the Internet. Instead, there are various FAQs and posts that address the topic. Some rules, however, are generally accepted and regarded as law by the citizens of the Internet, so you should abide by them whenever possible. These rules are as follows:

Don't ramble. Rambling about nothing in particular is annoying in most forms of communication, but in e-mail it's unbearable. Be as brief as possible without losing the content or proper tone of your message (messages that are too brief can seem curt or angry).

Don't rip on other people. Verbal communication has corrupted some of us. If you'd whisper something nasty about someone, you wouldn't think anyone could overhear, but sometimes they do. The same thing goes for e-mail. In fact, because e-mail can so easily end up in the wrong hands, a nasty e-mail message is more likely to "get back" to its subject than a whispered comment.

Respond promptly. Letting unanswered e-mail sit around doesn't benefit anyone. If you don't have an answer or reply for the sender yet, send an e-mail saying so.

Never e-mail something you wouldn't say in person. If you wouldn't say something to a person's face, don't say it via e-mail. First, it's a cop-out for physical confrontation, and second, that person has feelings, too.

Make sure the subject line really defines the content of your message. Nothing is more annoying than getting mail with a subject line called "Your Job Application Approval," and finding that it contains a Christmas greeting. If you have to send mail about miscellaneous things, make the subject line reflect that.

Re-read your message before pressing Send. Ninety percent of e-mail Netiquette no-no's result from the sender's failure to read the message after it's been written but before it's been sent. Reviewing your message after you've finished writing it will not only help you catch grammar and spelling errors, but will give you a glimpse of how your message will be read and understood by the reader.

Never send e-mail that you've received to someone else (unless you have permission). Let's say your friends Ken and Fred are online and you correspond with both of them. Don't send e-mail to Fred that Ken sent to you. Fred will think that he can't trust you with e-mail, and will be much less forthcoming in his future electronic correspondence with you. After all, what's to stop him from suspecting that you'll send those messages on to Ken? Then again, Ken and Fred might be forwarding your mail to each other....

Your words are a reflection on you. Once again, don't assume that the recipient is the only person who will ever see your message.

Treat everyone on the Internet as a human being. There are very few computer-based automatic messaging systems out there, and in all likelihood any e-mail that you send will eventually be read by a human somewhere. Even if you've never met someone face-to-face, remember that that person deserves to be treated with respect.

Don't use ALL CAPS. Internet dwellers call all caps "shouting," but to me it's just hard to read. Using all caps is probably the easiest way to get instant flames.

When replying, include a bit of the original message. Sending a message back to someone that consists of "No, I don't think so" can be just a bit confusing. This problem is even worse if you haven't replied immediately to the message in question.

Check e-mail at least once a day. I check my e-mail about four times a day while I'm working, and at least once a day when I'm not.

Don't make signatures longer than the content of the e-mail. If your message consists of one line, don't include a 10-line signature, no matter how cute it is.

Treat spoilers correctly. A "spoiler" is communication your recipient may not want to read because it divulges information the person might want to find out for himself or herself. For instance, be careful e-mailing comments about a movie you've seen unless you're positive your recipient has also seen it. Otherwise he or she might not want to know all about it.

If you want to send spoiler information, include a line that reads "Spoiler Info Below," and then insert about 20 hard returns so that the information is hidden down below the current screen. That way the recipient can read the information if he or she wants, but won't accidentally stumble upon it, finding out something like that in *Jurassic Park*, the dinosaurs did it.

Make sure your From line is correct. If your e-mail software lets you customize your From line, make sure it is totally correct, so that replies reach you. If you don't want replies to go to the address in the From line, make sure you indicate clearly where replies should go.

Don't enclose large files with your e-mail unless the recipient is expecting them. Many e-mail systems allocate a certain fixed amount of disk space for each user's incoming files and messages. When that amount overflows, either old files are deleted or the user is charged for the used disk space.

Bad Language Flame: You use the worst language I've ever heard...and I'm a Catholic schoolteacher!

Flame Flame: You have to be the most pathetic excuse for a flamer I have ever seen. Don't worry about running me off, because this is the last message you'll ever get from me, you moronic moron.

Don't assume the sex of the recipient. Because the majority of e-mail names consists of a first letter and a last name, it is often impossible to know your recipient's gender.

Don't forward received e-mail to newsgroups, mailing lists or other publicly accessible areas. This is for the most part a matter of common courtesy.

Avoid profanity and sexual innuendo. Nobody likes a sewer-mouth, especially from someone he or she has never met in person.

Moving On

All this stuff about correct and proper e-mail behavior is very constricting. So now that we've discussed some of the things that you *can't* (or at least shouldn't) do, in the next chapter we'll talk about how you *can* use e-mail to express yourself in many different and totally acceptable ways.

8

ACRONYMS, SMILEYS & SIGNATURES

As I mentioned back in Chapter 5, "Understanding E-Mail as a Medium," the best thing about e-mail is the lightning fast speed at which it can be created, sent and received. The only thing that slows down the process (besides a quick game of Marathon or Doom II in the middle of composition) is the time it takes to type an e-mail message, and, of course, the time it takes to read it.

If you're a touch typist (me? I'm a rattle-the-desk pound-typer) you don't have to worry too much about the first part, but it still takes a while to read, absorb and understand e-mail. (Of course, if your name is Evelyn Wood, you won't have a problem.)

Acronyms speed up the typing process, but slow down the reading process. Smileys slow down both the reading and typing processes. Then there are signatures, which for the most part eat up substantial amounts of e-mail effort on both the composing and receiving ends.

AOIEM (Acronym Overuse In E-Mail)

Whenever I read my Internet e-mail, I'm inundated with multiple sets of uppercase characters that look like words you used to make when you were losing at Scrabble—and there was no dictionary to prove you wrong. It all turns into some sort of bizarre coding system that Internet dwellers are supposed to understand inherently. If they don't, they are secretly ridiculed in private IRC rooms (Internet Relay Chat, where you can talk to people in real time through your Internet connection).

Common acronyms are acceptable in Internet e-mail usage, but anything beyond the norm is not. As time marches forward, more and more acronyms will be considered generally acceptable. The "IEMAATM" section later lists common and not-so-common acronyms.

A common paragraph for the over-acronymized might be as follows (acronyms are bold so you can spot them easily):

BTW, I had set up the entire backyard full of dominos when my **SO** came out and "tripped" over one of them. **IMHO**, I think she was **ROTFL** after she left. I told her, **CUL**, **BRB**, **TTFN**, and then went to go see a divorce lawyer. **FWIW**, I never did confront her **F2F** about the lawyer incident until I found out my **SO** had been to the same lawyer a few months earlier. **IOW**, **GMTA**, and we've been happy ever since.

This whole mess is interpreted as follows:

By The Way, I had set up the entire backyard full of dominos when my **Significant Other** came out and "tripped" over one of them. **In My Humble Opinion**, I think she was **Rolling On The Floor Laughing** after she left. I told her, **See You Later**, **Be Right Back**, **Ta Ta For Now**, and then went to go see a divorce lawyer. **For What It's Worth**, I didn't confront her **Face to Face** about the lawyer incident until I found out my **Significant Other** had been to the same lawyer a few months earlier. **In Other Words**, **Great Minds Think Alike**, and we've been happy ever since.

In this case, and in many others, acronyms add little substance to the message. In fact, when used under the wrong conditions, they are actually more confusing than useful.

WTUA (When To Use Acronyms)

When used under the right conditions, however, acronyms are cool, entertaining and a huge sign of your Internet intelligence. These conditions include the following:

- *When the recipient(s) knows what the acronym means.* There are several people who communicate with me primarily through e-mail, and when I send them messages, I'll use several not-so-familiar acronyms that I know *they* know.

- *When you want to show your Internet Hipness Quotient (IHQ).* Of course, the acronyms you use must be easy to interpret and recognize. Otherwise, you'll be considered an FFC (Freak From Cyberspace).

- *When you are using a long phrase repeatedly.* The first time you use a phrase like "Internet Hipness Quotient," write out the entire thing and then put the acronym in parentheses, as shown above. After that, you can use just the acronym throughout the rest of your message, and your IHQ will soar.

If there's an acronym you want to use only once, and you have to explain what it means, don't bother using it. The one exception to this rule occurs when you are communicating with a first-time Internet dweller (a *newbie*) and you want to use a well-known acronym. In that case go ahead and use it, because newbies will need a thorough explanation to help them understand what the heck you're saying with all those capital letters.

IEMAATM (Internet E-Mail Acronyms & Their Meanings)

The bold entries on this list are more common than the non-bold ones. Of course, just because I think some of these acronyms are common doesn't mean that anyone in the state of Vermont (VT) has ever heard of them, so don't assume that everyone on the Internet knows what they mean. This list is by no means complete.

Acronym	Decoded
AAT	And Another Thing
ARPWIP	Are You Pondering What I'm Pondering?
BRB	**Be Right Back**
BTW	**By The Way**
BWB	Be Write Back (a variation for authors)
CMIO	Crying My Eyes Out
CUL	See You Later
CUL8R	See You Later
F2F	Face to Face
FWIW	For What It's Worth
FYA	For Your Amusement
FYI	**For Your Information**
GD&R	Grin, Duck & Run
GMTA	**Great Minds Think Alike**
HHOK	Ha Ha Only Kidding
IMHO	**In My Humble Opinion**
IMO	In My Opinion
IOW	In Other Words

IRC	Internet Relay Chat
L8R	Later
LOL	Laughing Out Loud
OBO	Or Best Offer
OBTW	Oh By The Way
OIC	Oh I See
OTF	On The Floor (laughing)
PC	Politically Correct
PMFBI	Pardon Me For Butting In
PMFJI	Pardon Me For Jumping In
ROTFL	**Rolling On The Floor Laughing (also ROFL)**
RSN	Real Soon Now
RTFM	**Read The Freakin' Manual**
RTM	Read The Manual
SO	Significant Other
SWF	Single White Female
TANSTAAFL	There Ain't No Such Thing As A Free Lunch
TIA	Thanks In Advance
TNX	**Thanks**
TTFN	Ta Ta For Now
WB	Welcome Back
WRT	With Respect To
WTG	**Way To Go**
YMMV	Your Mileage May Vary
YW&D	Yakko, Wakko & Dot

Smileys :-)

Smileys are little faces created with various combinations of colons and paragraph symbols to represent different expressions. Turn this book clockwise 90 degrees to see the smiling smiley face:

:-)

This is an unhappy smiley face:

:-(

This is a sly, winking smiley face:

;-)

So by using different characters from your keyboard you can create almost limitless combinations of smiley faces. And yes, they're called smileys even if they're frowning.

Smileys are probably the most fun you can have online when you're starting out. Overall, their use is frowned upon by most of the educational institution types who have had Net access for several years. In fact, until recently a hard-and-fast definition for a newbie was as follows:

If the number of smileys in any given message is an integer greater than zero, the user is a newbie.

Now, with millions of Internet dwellers and hoppers, the use of smileys has taken on a whole new meaning. Using a smiley no longer indicates that you are a newbie, but rather that you aren't from the "old school" of Interneters.

Remember that too many smileys will make your text appear too giddy. The absolute limit is a smiley with each paragraph, and even that's rather excessive.

Not Everyone Understands Smileys   Contrary to what some people believe, smileys do not serve as some sort of universal textual gauge for emotion. Some people really have no idea what the heck they are. A friend of mine recently sent a resumé to a high-end electronics component producer, and in the cover letter he included several smileys of assorted design to emphasize various statements.

At first it seemed to work: he was called in for an interview almost immediately. When he sat down in front of the gruff old interviewer, he noticed his cover letter on the man's lap with several inked markings. Seizing the moment, he commented, "Did you enjoy reading my cover letter?"

The interviewer responded, "I would've enjoyed it much more if your typewriter didn't have a broken open parenthesis key. It took me a great deal of time to figure out where to place all those parentheses."

What Use Do Smileys Have? :-(

Smileys are a simple, effective way to add expression to your text. If your text is dull or boring, a smiley stuck in the right place can liven up your message. Smileys can also indicate when you're kidding or being sarcastic about something. A statement like this would normally be construed as just another fact in your daily life:

I'm going to see my Uncle Arthur this weekend.

But if you spruce it up with a smiley, it becomes something you've wanted to do for a long time, and you just can't wait:

I'm going to see my Uncle Arthur this weekend. :-)

Now everyone will know that you like your uncle, and that you positively enjoy his company.

The Smiley List

The following list is by no means complete, but it does show some of the fun you can have with smileys. The interpretations of each smiley are my own, and may not be interpreted the same way universally.

Smiley	Name	Description
o :-)	Angelic	Sure, you would never do that.
=:-)	Bart Simpson	There is no relevance to using the Bart Simpson smiley.
d:-)	Baseball Fanatic	Frowns during a strike.
:>)	Beak-Nose	Not the most flattering thing you can type.
:^)	Big Schnozz	You prefer the term "distinctive" when it comes to discussing that mutant growth in the middle of your face.

P-)	Black Beard	"I bought my software...really."
:-) X	Bow Ties Are In	Not really, but they do let more of that polyester sheen (from your shirt) show.
& :-)	Bow-in-Hair	Or bone-in-hair, depending on how you look at it.
:-Q	Chain Smoker	Lung cancer is really an okay way to die a slow, painful death.
*<:o)	Clown Dude	
8-)	Coke Bottle Eyes	Or really really big contact lenses.
- -)	Cyclops	Not the most practical smiley I've seen.
<:-)	Dunce	Stupid is as stupid types.
}:-)	Eddie Munster	You've got great hair...for a vampire.
~~:-(	Flamed	A few thousand nasty comments have been tossed your way.
::-)	Four Eyes	If your readers get this right away, they are rather cool themselves, but not as cool as you for sending it.
$-)	Greedy	
:-<	Grief Incarnate	You're so upset that even a big bag of lollipops with happy smileys on them wouldn't cheer you up.
:-)	Happy	The subject matter delights you.
{:-)	Happy Toupee	Your hair piece looks really bad and obvious, but at least you don't blind innocent passersby on a sunny day anymore.

:->	Happy With Thyself	You've made some witty statement and want to make sure everyone reading your note understands that you think it's witty.
:-I	Have a Day	You're so nonplussed you might as well be subtraction incarnate.
B-)	Horn Rimmer	You think that they make you look intelligent, not dweebish.
/:///	Invisible Man	As a result of unforeseeable circumstances, you have become invisible. It could happen.
:-D	Laughing	Something is disturbingly funny, so much that your kidneys may explode.
:-q	Michael Jordon	Your tongue hangs about three inches out of your mouth when you (1) sky over the D for a slam or (2) try to hit a wiffle ball.
:-t	Moody	Usually indicative that you aren't in the mood for anything more light-hearted than discussing Bosnia.
:-E	Mutant Vampire	One too many fangs, but your victims don't seem to mind.
:-F	Mutant Vampire	After losing a fight, and consequently, a fang.
:-X	Mute	Or sealed and locked lips, swallowed the key (I've always thought that was silly, since you can't...).
:-{	Nasty Mustache	If you have one of those really cool (ha!) twisty long mustaches.

B:-)	On Forehead	"Anyone see my sunglasses?"
:-/	Perplexed	Confused and bewildered, like the way you felt the first time you heard about the Internet.
:-P	Phhhbbbbbbbt	Sticking out your tongue at the recipient. Something that is quite acceptable via e-mail yet frowned upon in actual conversation. And you don't have to discreetly wipe any saliva from your face when you're done.
:-?	Pipe-smoker	Lung cancer is bad. Lip cancer is good.
#-)	Plastered	Had a little too much of dat ole hi-powered whiskey-soda.
K:-)	Propeller-Head	You're a nerd and proud of it.
:-(	Sad	Something, alas, is amiss. Woe is you.
*<:-)	Santa	Great for the two weeks before Christmas only.
O-)	Scuba Diver	You are an aquatic buff, and want to squeeze this information into the conversation somehow.
:-O	Shocked	Something is just totally unbelievable.
:-*	Smoocher	You REALLY like this person.
[:-)	Stereo Man	If you aren't plugged in, you might as well not exist.
:-]	Stupid Grin	"Uh, I'm not sure why I'm smilin', but, uh..."

:,-)	Tears of Joy	So happy about something it makes you cry. I *still* don't get it.
:-&	Tongue-Tied	You are, for a change, silent.
:-()	Too Much Lipstick	"Blot me!"
:-) B	Topless	You like being provocative to the point of disrobing.
=):-)	Uncle Sammy	
{:-(	Unhappy Toupee	Not only does your hair piece look atrocious, but your scalp is starting to recede.
:,-(	Unparalleled Grief	You've just found out that this week's *Mad About You* is a repeat.
;-)	Winker	You're a sly dog, you know it, and you want your reader to know at as well.

Signatures

A signature is any combination of characters that you use to close an e-mail message. Many Internet e-mailers have several signatures.

This is one of mine that I change as needed:

```
/---------------------------------\
/ /----------------------------------\ \
/ /Ted Alspach, World Famous Author(TM) of:\ \
/ /                                          \ \
/ /       "The Macworld Illustrator 5.0/5.5 Bible"  \ \
/ /    "The Complete Idiot's Guide to QuarkXPress"    \ \
/ /    "The Complete Idiot's Guide to Photoshop"      \ \
\ <         "Internet E-Mail Quick Tour"             / /
\ \          "The Complete Idiot's Guide to          / /
\ \               Word for the Mac"                  / /
\ \          "Illustrator Filter Finesse"           / /
\ \             (w/ Jennifer Alspach)               / /
\ \----------------------------------/ /
\---------------------------------/
```

Here's another one:

```
|    Ted Alspach      ||       "Well, at least we have
|    Toulouse@crl.com ||       someone to blame for the
|    Toulouse@aol.com ||          Cardinals losing now."
```

And here's a subdued one that I use sometimes:

```
~Tools^^
```

A signature can have anything you want inside it. Some e-mail software has a signature function built right into it. If yours doesn't, you can use a program like QuicKeys or FastKeys to create a macro that will type it for you.

Here are a few examples of other signatures that use the various
ASCII characters to form pictures:

```
Keep cool and _\|/_ Have a good weekend!
                {o o}
=============================ooO=(_)=Ooo=====================================
                  This is a smoke-free .sig
```

```
"Frankly my dear,        /|   /|  |             |  "That I can
 I don't give a damn!"   ||_||  |   V O T E Trivia Ralph  |    not do."
—Clark Gable             /  O O\__    most likely to      |   -Marlon
                        /        \                         |    Brando
"Normally I would      /          \     _____   |  The Godfather
have taken cocaine."  /  _         \     [fill in the blank] | 
 —Dennis Hopper      /  |\____\     \    -------------------------
   1986 Oscars      /   | | | |\_____/     ||
                   /    \|_|_|/    |        ||  "This is this." ——Robert De Niro
                  / /  \         |_____| ||
                 / |   | /|      |        _||      "Billy Crystal?- I
                 | |   |//       |_____    —|      crap bigger than him!"
           *_    | |_|_|_|       |            —|       —Jack Palance
         * — _-\ _ \    //       |          \-/          1992 Oscars
         /  _  \\ _ // |      /  "You're trying to seduce me, Mrs. Robinson...
       * /  \_ /- | - |       |    aren't you?"
        *  ___ c_c_c_C/ \C_c_c_c_____—Dustin Hoffman, The Graduate
"I do an Oscar show every five years to remind people out there I'm alive."
---Paul Newman, 1991 Oscars
```

```
(Moo,)_____


_____                              (__)      (Moo, Moo!)
                                         (oo)    O (————)
Matthew W. Hansen              / ————\/   o
_____                   /  |     ||
Matthew.W.Hansen@uwrf.edu    *  ||———||
                               ~~    ~~
University of Wisconsin River Falls  —  Academic Computing
```

```
    _____
 (_)                     ) "The only difference between a saint and a
 |      The Saint        |  sinner is that every saint has a past and
 |   saint@ctron.com     |  every sinner has a future."
 |  _____|_             Oscar Wilde
 \_)_____)
```

```
                       |
 (_\      /_)          | "From the beginning I knew that there's
  \_\    /_/           | nothing wrong with you that I can't
   \_\/_/              | fix with my hands."
   /  _/  )            |        -Batman, Batman: Hunt the Dark Knight
  / /(\/  )            | "Pretty sure."
  \/  /_/              |        -Indiana Jones, Indiana Jones and
   \ / /               |           the Last Crusade
   | | |               | "Jesus Christ, Powell! He could be a
                       | f*cking bartender for all we know!!!"
                       |        -Deputy Chief of Police Dwayne T.
                       |           Robinson, Die Hard
   Ross Johnson : johns224@cps.msu.edu — Worshipper of
        Frank Miller.
```

Moving On

Now you know how to spice up your e-mail with all sorts of hilarious acronyms, smileys and signatures. Just the sort of thing that the people who created the Internet in the first place were hoping wouldn't happen: enjoyment.

The next chapter will explain some of the amazing things e-mail can do, especially if Internet e-mail is the limit of what your Internet package provides for you.

9

MAILING LISTS, NEWSGROUPS & FILES

E-mail *can* be a spectator sport. If your major goal in life is to read and receive tons of e-mail, that can easily be arranged. On the other hand, you can also take part in more interactive services, such as newsgroups and mailing lists, even if e-mail is the only Internet service you have.

Junk E-Mail

If you make your electronic address easily available, chances are good that you'll find yourself on someone's electronic address list before long. This means that you'll start to receive all sorts of notices, mailings and information that until then had appeared only in your mailbox at home.

I get this junk e-mail from a variety of sources, including a magazine vendor who sends 10-page mail "letters" that list a variety of special deals. I've gotten junk e-mail from several software manufacturers, individuals who want help with electronic petitions, organizations who want donations, other organizations asking for participants, and still other organizations who want nothing more than someone to read the mindless drivel they send out.

If you get more Internet junk e-mail than you can deal with, you can usually ask these organizations (through an e-mail reply) to remove your address from their list, and they will do so at once. Occasionally you might have to be more persistent (when I'm really annoyed, I'll send mail twice a day until they reply telling me that they'll remove my name). The aforementioned magazine company told me they couldn't remove my name from their list. I ended up e-mailing removal requests every time I logged on (about six times a day), and they managed to change their policy for me. I guess they finally understood what a pain it was to get unsolicited e-mail that they didn't want to read.

> **Commercialization on the Internet** Long-time denizens of the Internet feel very strongly that the Internet should not be used for commercialization purposes. The Net's primary function, they contend, is to exchange information, not commerce. They have a nice aesthetic point. But in reality, as more and more businesses gain access to the Internet, business transactions will become more common, and commercialization will inevitably result.

As Internet addresses become more available, more and more people will start receiving junk mail. I know that one day I'll see Ed McMahon's face at the top of a particularly long Internet e-mail message—then we'll know we're all in trouble.

Mailing Lists

If you love getting e-mail, subscribing to a mailing list (or to several) is a way for you to get to heaven without getting splattered on the highway by an out-of-control semi. When I first learned how to subscribe to mailing lists, I went crazy and subscribed to about 10 of them. Then I got burned out...really fast. Now I subscribe to only one.

A *mailing list* is a list of e-mail addresses whose owners share an interest in a certain topic, like 64-bit video games, foosball or Bloom

County. All mailing-list participants can send topic-related messages to a central address (technically, it's a mail server, but there's no need for us to be technical here, right?), and that message is automatically forwarded to *everyone* on that mailing list.

To become part of a mailing list, you'll need to subscribe to it. Each mailing list has slightly different policies, but sending empty e-mail with "subscribe" as the subject is usually enough to gain a subscription. By the same token, if you decide not to continue with your subscription, sending e-mail with the word "Unsubscribe" in it will remove your name from the mailing list.

Once you've subscribed to the mailing list, you'll start receiving boatloads of mail from other people on the list. No person has access to the names on the mailing list (except maybe the system administrator), so subscribers never know the identities of the people reading their message. In other words, when you send mail to the server address, it will end up in the e-mail boxes of all the other subscribers, without your ever knowing who is reading it.

Getting a List of Lists

Of course, all this talk about mailing lists does you no good if you don't know what to subscribe to in the first place. There are actually two different types of mailing lists—Internet mailing lists and Bitnet mailing lists—though they both work pretty much the same way. For a list of Internet mailing lists, send e-mail to mail-server@BLOOM-PICAYUNE.MIT.EDU, and include the following in the message text:

Send /pub/usenet/news.lists/mail/mailing-lists/part1

There are several parts. To get the other parts, change part1 to part2, then part3, etc. The number of parts is continuously increasing, but you'll know how many parts there are by the heading in the message (part 1 of 10, etc.).

To get a list of Bitnet mailing lists, send e-mail to LISTSERVE@BITNIC.bitnet with nothing in the subject line and the following in the message text:

LIST GLOBAL

A nice thing about Bitnet mailing lists is that you can specify what type of lists you're looking for, by adding a slash and the topic you're interested in. For instance, if I wanted info on e-mail, my message text would read as follows:

LIST GLOBAL /E-MAIL

The results of my search (sent back to me via e-mail) look like the following:

```
Excerpt from the LISTSERV lists known to LISTSERV@BITNIC on 27 Dec 1994 10:16
Search string: E-MAIL
*********************************************************************
* To subscribe, send mail to LISTSERV@LISTSERV.NET with the following *
* command in the text (not the subject) of your message:             *
*                                                                    *
*                      SUBSCRIBE listname                            *
*                                                                    *
* Replace 'listname' with the name in the first column of the table. *
*********************************************************************
Network-wide ID  Full address and list description

CAR-ENG         CAR-ENG@CSEARN.BITNET
                CAROLINA - E-mail news weekly

EM-NSP-ITA      EM-NSP@ICNUCEVM.BITNET
                List of the E-Mail Network Service Providers in Italy

EMTF-L          EMTF-L@NIHLIST.BITNET
                Government-wide E-mail Task Force

GC-L            GC-L@URIACC.BITNET
                GC-L, Global Classroom: International Students E-mail Debate
```

```
ICONS            ICONS@UMDD.BITNET
                 ICONS E-Mail Discussion Group

KAIROS           KAIROS@UTCVM.BITNET
                 KAIROS E-Mail Distribution Service

MITBAY           MITBAY@MITVMA.BITNET
                 MIT Northern California Club E-MAIL NETWORK

MITCHGO          MITCHGO@MITVMA.BITNET
                 MIT Club of Chicago E-MAIL NETWORK

MITDC            MITDC@MITVMA.BITNET
                 MIT Club of Washington DC E-Mail Network

MITNY            MITNY@MITVMA.BITNET
                 MIT Club of New York E-Mail Network

MITSECT          MITSECT@MITVMA.BITNET
                 MIT Class Secretaries E-Mail Network

MITWCREW         MITWCREW@MITVMA.BITNET
                 MIT Varsity Women's Crew E-MAIL Network

MIT1961          MIT1961@MITVMA.BITNET
                 MIT Class of 1961 E-Mail Network

MIT1962          MIT1962@MITVMA.BITNET
                 MIT Class of 1962 e-mail network

MIT1964          MIT1964@MITVMA.BITNET
                 MIT Class of 1964 E-Mail Network

MIT1966          MIT1966@MITVMA.BITNET
                 MIT Class of 1966 e-mail network

MIT1970          MIT1970@MITVMA.BITNET
                 MIT Class of 1970 E-Mail Network

MIT1972          MIT1972@MITVMA.BITNET
                 MIT Class of 1972 e-mail network

MIT1973          MIT1973@MITVMA.BITNET
                 MIT Class of 1973 E-Mail Network
```

```
MIT1976          MIT1976@MITVMA.BITNET
                 MIT Class of 1976 E-Mail Network

MIT1987          MIT1987@MITVMA.BITNET
                 MIT Class of 1987 E-Mail Network

MIT1988          MIT1988@MITVMA.BITNET
                 MIT Class of 1988 E-Mail Network

MIT1991          MIT1991@MITVMA.BITNET
                 MIT Class of 1991 E-Mail Network

MIT1992          MIT1992@MITVMA.BITNET
                 MIT Class of 1992 E-Mail Network

MIT1993          MIT1993@MITVMA.BITNET
                 MIT Class of 1993 E-Mail Network
```

Because all the Bitnet mailing lists are automated, you follow the same procedure (shown at the top of the list) to subscribe to each of them.

Mailing List Netiquette

If you do decide to join a mailing list, remember that thousands of people will be receiving every letter you send (as well as many other letters) through this correspondence. For this reason, mailing lists require careful attention to Netiquette. In addition to the rules listed in Chapter 7, there are a few other considerations to keep in mind when writing to a mailing list:

- Don't send a message just to announce that you agree with a statement, unless you have something else to say as well.

- Don't flame anyone through a mailing list message. Send your flame directly to the flamee.

- Always include your e-mail address in your signature when sending a message to a mailing list, so readers can contact you without sending mail to the entire list.
- Don't start up a "conversation" that is unrelated to the topic.
- If you become involved in an exchange with one other person on the list, and this correspondence lasts several messages, continue your exchange through private Internet e-mail, not through the mailing list.
- Wait 1–2 weeks after you subscribe to a list before sending e-mail to the mailing list. Read what others are saying first, so you understand the tone, knowledge base and depth of the topic.
- Make your subject line as descriptive as possible, especially when replying. You don't want a subject that says "Re: eggnog recipe" with a message text that comments on the political upheaval in your favorite South American country.

Don't Get Carried Away   There are thousands of mailing lists, covering a wide variety of subjects. If you subscribed to all of them, you'd receive so much mail that you wouldn't have time to read a fraction of it, and you wouldn't be able to delete messages as fast as you would receive them.

The point of all this? Subscribe to one mailing list at a time. If you find yourself constantly deleting messages from one mailing list, you might want to stop subscribing to it right away. In addition, if your Internet service provider charges you a per-piece e-mail charge, you could easily have to get a second mortgage, etc., in no time.

Organized Mailing Lists

Some mailing lists (the ones that I prefer) are lucky enough to have an editor. This person will sift through and edit the contents of the list, and then send out a complete "batch" of messages combined into one or several parts. This is a wonderful thing. Instead of getting messages as they trickle in slowly, members receive a chunk of organized mail they can browse through at their leisure.

If you belong to such a mailing list, remember that all rules of mailing-list Netiquette still apply, and that your message may be subject to censoring or editing (though I have rarely seen either happen). You won't receive as much e-mail this way, either.

Newsgroups by E-Mail

Newsgroups are collections of messages related to a specific topic of interest. You can gain direct access to a newsgroup if you have full Internet access (or even a limited connection through America Online or one of the other commercial services).

If you don't have direct access to newsgroups, you can still subscribe to several of them, in the same way as you subscribe to mailing lists. To get a list of the newsgroups available through e-mail, send a message to mail-server@BLOOM-PICAYUNE.MIT.EDU. Include the following in your message:

> Send /pub/usenet/news.announce.newusers/mail/news-gateways/part1

If you decide to subscribe to a newsgroup, send mail to *(name of newsgroup)*-request@address. Your text message should read "subscribe *(name of newsgroup) (your first name) (your last name)."*

Files by E-Mail

If you want to retrieve files just by using e-mail, various services can help you do this. Any file you can save or move around on your computer system on a hard drive or a floppy can be sent to others across the Internet via e-mail. It is always better if you know exactly *where* the files are stored (the "file server" location as well as the exact directory where your specific file is located) before you set out to get them, but even if you don't have all that information, there are ways to retrieve them.

FTPmail is the easiest of these services to use, especially (once again) if you already know exactly where the file is located. FTP stands for File Transfer Protocol, a standard for sending and receiving files across the Internet. Send your message to either ftpmail@decwrl.dec.com (Massachusetts) or ftpmail@sunsite.unc.edu (North Carolina), depending on which is closer to you.

Leave the subject line blank, and include the following in the message text (where *ftp.site* is the name of the FTP site, *dir/dir/dir* is the path to the file, and *filename* is the name of the file you want):

Open *ftp.site*
cd *dir/dir/dir*
get *filename*
quit

For instance, if you knew that a file called marathon0.0demo.cpt.hqx could be found at mac.archive.umich.edu in the /mac/game/demo directory, your message would look like this:

To: ftpmail@sunsite.unc.edu
Subject:

Open mac.archive.umich.edu
cd /mac/game/demo
get marathon0.0demo.cpt.hqx
quit

And you would receive the file—eventually. This process takes much longer than standard FTPing but you don't have to be tied up while the file is transferred.

If you know the file's location, but aren't sure of its name or directory, you can send a request. This can also take a long time to process. For instance, if I were to request the name of the files in the /mac/game/demo directory at mac.archive.umich.edu, I would send mail to ftpmail@sunsite.unc.edu with the following message:

Open mac.archive.umich.edu
dir /mac/game/demo
quit

This would return a list of all the files in that directory, including their sizes and "proper" names.

Moving On

This chapter probably whetted your appetite for more Internet services. The next chapter will introduce you to the additional services on the Internet that you can access if you have a full connection.

10

BEYOND E-MAIL

E-mail is the core of Internet communications, but its capabilities are limited. Many of the Internet's more sophisticated features are beyond e-mail's scope. But although you can't gain access through e-mail to the more complex services of the Internet, e-mail itself (or at least the notion of e-mail) is a necessary component of all of these services.

This chapter serves as your introduction to Telnet, FTP, newsgroups, the World Wide Web and Gopher, all of which sound really bizarre until you get to know what they're about. Then they don't just *sound* bizarre anymore....

Telnet: Remote Control

Telnet lets you log onto other computers as if they were your own. As one of the first major Internet services, Telnet has been primarily a command-line interface, though various newly created Windows and Mac software products hide that nasty text screen and do most of the command typing for you.

You can use Telnet to access all sorts of information, from the Library of Congress to sports schedules to up-to-date weather information. Better do it fast though—Telnet services are slowly disappearing, and being replaced by...

The World Wide Web

The World Wide Web is one of the fastest growing areas of the Internet. The Web (as we Net people refer to it) is composed of thousands of documents known as "pages." Every page consists not only of text and graphics (even movies), but "links" to other pages, in the form of underlined words or graphics. By clicking on a link (or selecting it with a text-based connection), you can jump from page to page instantly. The links that join the pages together are the basis for the web analogy.

Figure 10-1: *The World Wide Web, showing a "page" from WWW.vmedia.com using Netscape Navigator software.*

You can gain access to the Web through a standard UNIX connection, or if you have a SLIP or PPP account, you can use specialized software designed just for navigating the Web. The most popular software is NCSA's Mosaic, followed by Netscape (which is gaining on the leader). Both software packages can be downloaded at various...

FTP Sites

FTP stands for File Transfer Protocol. It's one of the standards on the Internet that allows files to travel from one location to the next quickly and easily. Chapter 9 describes how to use FTP through e-mail, but FTPing files is much easier if you have full Internet access.

If you have a text-based carrier, you can gain access to a file server by typing the command "ftp" and then the server's location. If you need to locate files, a service called Archie will find titles related to your search parameters. There are also special software packages (such as Fetch, the most popular one) that allow you to download files easily from Mac and Windows systems.

If all you want are documents or information, you might try using...

Gopher

Gopher is a service that helps you along as you search for information on a specific subject. Whereas the World Wide Web lets you jump around from link to link, Gopher takes you right to the source.

In addition, Gopher makes better use of its time than FTP. Instead of opening a connection and continuously using up valuable "bandwidth" on the Internet, Gopher opens one connection at a time, and quickly zips from site to site in search of your topic. Sometimes you'll get a document; other times it will locate an FTP site or a Web page. And sometimes the search will produce references to various...

Newsgroups

As mentioned in Chapter 9, newsgroups are collections of messages related to a specific topic of interest. Thousands of newsgroups cover almost every topic imaginable, from comic books to computer graphics. Anyone can read posted newsgroup messages, and anyone can reply to them. See Chapter 9 for more info on working with newsgroups through e-mail.

Moving On

E-mail is your link to all these services, because it is your first and primary means of identification. When you post a message to a newsgroup, your e-mail address is automatically included. When you access an FTP site—and you log in as "anonymous"—you'll be asked to provide your e-mail address anyway, as a password.

In other words, e-mail is the foundation of all you'll do on the Internet. It's your ticket to communication, and the basis for everything else. And as important as it is already, it is not even close to its ultimate worth. As more and more businesses, people and organizations "get connected," the benefits and value of Internet e-mail will skyrocket.

Internet e-mail has the potential to be the leading form of business communication within just a few short years. Think back five years, when most businesses had a fax machine, but there were those that didn't. Annoying, wasn't it? The same can now be said for e-mail addresses. Get an Internet e-mail address and you'll stay within that elusive loop.

APPENDIX A
INTERNET E-MAIL SERVICES

Internet Service Providers

If you're looking for an Internet service provider to set you up with an Internet e-mail account, the following should provide you with the information you need. Find a provider that services your area code, then call the listed phone number for more information.

The information in this list was gathered from Pdial, a listing of Internet Service providers maintained by Peter Kaminski. You can get a complete file, listing prices, local access availability and more, by sending e-mail to info-deli-server@netcom.com that contains the phrase "Send PDIAL."

Internet Service Provider	Area Code Serviced	Phone Number
a2i communications	408	408-293-8078
Anomaly - Rhode Island's Gateway to the Internet	401, 508	401-273-4669
APK - Public Access UNI Site	216	216-481-9428
CAPCON Library Network	202, 301, 410, 703	202-331-5771
Colorado SuperNet, Inc.	303, 719, 800	303-273-3471

Internet Service Provider	Area Code Serviced	Phone Number
Communications Accessibles Montreal	514	514-923-2102
Community News Service	303, 719, 800	719-579-9120
CONCERT-CONNECT	704, 919	919-248-1999
Cooperative Library Agency for Systems and Services	800	800-488-4559
CR Laboratories Dialup Internet Access	415, 510, 602, 707, 800	415-381-2800
CTS Network Services (CTSNET)	619	619-593-9597
DIAL n' CERF or DIAL n' CERF AYC or DIAL n' CERF USA	213, 310, 415, 510, 619, 714, 818, 800	800-876-2373
Eskimo North	206	206-367-7457
Express Access - Online Communications Service	202, 301, 410, 703, 908	800-546-2010
Grebyn Corporation	202, 301, 703	703-281-2194
Halcyon	206	206-955-1050
HoloNet	510	510-704-0160
IDS World Network	401	401-884-7856
Institute for Global Communications/IGC Networks	415, 800	415-442-0220
John von Neumann Computer Network	800	800-35-TIGER
Maestro	212, 718	212-240-9600

Internet Service Provider	Area Code Serviced	Phone Number
Merit Network, Inc.	313, 517, 616, 906	313-764-9430
Meta Network	703, 202, 301	703-243-6622
MindVOX	212, 718	212-989-2418
MSen	313	313-998-4562
MV Communications, Inc.	603	603-429-2223
NEARnet	508, 603, 617	617-873-8730
NeoSoft's Sugar Land Unix	713	713-438-4964
Netcom Online Communication Services	206, 213, 310, 408, 415, 503, 510, 619, 818, 916	408-554-UNIX
North Shore Access	617, 508	617-593-3110
Northwest Nexus Inc.	206	206-455-3505
NovaLink	508	800-274-2814
OARnet	614, 513, 419, 216, 800	614-292-8100
Old Colorado City Communications	719	719-632-4848
PANIX Public Access Unix	212, 718	212-877-4854
Portal System	408, 415	408-973-9111
PREPnet	215, 412, 717, 814	412-268-7870
PUCnet Computer Connections	403	403-448-1901

Internet Service Provider	Area Code Serviced	Phone Number
Telerama Public Access Internet	412	412-481-3505
Texas Metronet	214	214-401-2800
UUnorth	416, 519, 613	416-225-8649
Vnet Internet Access, Inc	704	704-374-0779
Whole Earth 'Lectronic Link	415	415-332-4335
World	617	617-739-0202
Wyvern Technologies, Inc.	804	804-622-4289

Commercial Service Providers

The following lists the names and phone numbers of the major commercial services (all of which provide Internet e-mail service). If you want to set up an online account with any of these services, call them for more information.

Provider	Phone Number
America Online	800-827-6364
AT&T Mail	800-624-5672
CompuServe	800-848-8199
Delphi	800-544-4005
eWorld	800-775-4556
GEnie	800-638-9396
MCI Mail	800-444-6245
Prodigy	800-776-3449

APPENDIX B
MAIL GATEWAY & DOMAIN REFERENCE

Mail Gateway Reference

More often than not, you'll send or receive Internet e-mail to or from a commercial online service provider, such as America Online or CompuServe. The following is a listing of the "domains" that follow the user ID and the @ symbol.

Service	Domain Name	Mail to DogHarvey Looks Like:
America Online	aol.com	DogHarvey@aol.com
Applelink	applelink.apple.com	DogHarvey@applelink.apple.com
AT&T Mail	attmail.com	DogHarvey@attmail.com
CompuServe	compuServe.com	15145.9987@compuserve.com*
Delphi	delphi.com	DogHarvey@delphi.com
eWorld	eworld.com	DogHarvey@eworld.com
GEnie	genie.geis.com	DogHarvey@genie.geis.com
MCI Mail	mcimail.com	DogHarvey@mcimail.com
Prodigy	prodigy.com	DogHarvey@prodigy.com

* User IDs on CompuServe have a comma in the middle, which is always changed to a dot (.) before sending e-mail across the Internet. *Don't* change the comma when sending e-mail from one CompuServe e-mail address to another.

Domain Reference

Following is a guide to the three-letter extensions that appear at the end of most Internet e-mail addresses:

Extension	Meaning
.com	Commercial
.edu	Educational
.gov	Government
.mil	Military
.net	Network Resource
.org	Organization

APPENDIX C
COUNTRY CODES

If you want to send e-mail to a person or business located in another country, you will need to insert a specific country code at the end of that e-mail address. The following is a list of foreign country codes:

Afghanistan (Islamic St.)	.af	Belgium	.be
Albania	.al	Belize	.bz
Algeria	.dz	Benin	.bj
American Samoa	.as	Bermuda	.bm
Andorra	.ad	Bhutan	.bt
Angola, Republic of	.ao	Bolivia	.bo
Anguilla	.ai	Bosnia-Herzegovina	.ba
Antarctica	.aq	Botswana	.bw
Antigua & Barbuda	.ag	Bouvet Island	.bv
Argentina	.ar	Brazil	.br
Armenia	.am	British Indian O. Terr.	.io
Aruba	.aw	Brunei Darussalam	.bn
Australia	.au	Bulgaria	.bg
Austria	.at	Burkina Faso	.bf
Azerbaijan	.az	Burundi	.bi
Bahamas	.bs	Cambodia	.kh
Bahrain	.bh	Cameroon	.cm
Bangladesh	.bd	Canada	.ca
Barbados	.bb	Cape Verde	.cv
Belarus	.by	Cayman Islands	.ky

Central African Rep.	.cf	Finland	.fi
Chad	.td	France (European Ter.)	.fx
Chile	.cl	France	.fr
China	.cn	French Southern Terr.	.tf
Christmas Island	.cx	Gabon	.ga
Cocos (Keeling) Isl.	.cc	Gambia	.gm
Colombia	.co	Georgia	.ge
Comoros	.km	Germany	.de
Congo	.cg	Ghana	.gh
Cook Islands	.ck	Gibraltar	.gi
Costa Rica	.cr	Great Britain (UK)	.gb
Croatia	.hr	Greece	.gr
Cuba	.cu	Greenland	.gl
Cyprus	.cy	Grenada	.gd
Czech Republic	.cz	Guadeloupe (Fr.)	.gp
Czechoslovakia	.cs	Guam (US)	.gu
Denmark	.dk	Guatemala	.gt
Djibouti	.dj	Guinea	.gn
Dominica	.dm	Guinea Bissau	.gw
Dominican Republic	.do	Guyana (Fr.)	.gf
East Timor	.tp	Guyana	.gy
Ecuador	.ec	Haiti	.ht
Egypt	.eg	Heard & McDonald Isl.	.hm
El Salvador	.sv	Honduras	.hn
Equatorial Guinea	.gq	Hong Kong	.hk
Eritrea	.er	Hungary	.hu
Estonia	.ee	Iceland	.is
Ethiopia	.et	India	.in
Falkland Isl. (Malvinas)	.fk	Indonesia	.id
Faroe Islands	.fo	Iran	.ir
Fiji	.fj	Iraq	.iq

Ireland	.ie	Marshall Islands	.mh
Israel	.il	Martinique	.mq
Italy	.it	Mauritania	.mr
Ivory Coast	.ci	Mauritius	.mu
Jamaica	.jm	Mayotte	.yt
Japan	.jp	Mexico	.mx
Jordan	.jo	Micronesia	.fm
Kazachstan	.kz	Moldova	.md
Kenya	.ke	Monaco	.mc
Kiribati	.ki	Mongolia	.mn
Korea, North	.kp	Montserrat	.ms
Korea, South	.kr	Morocco	.ma
Kuwait	.kw	Mozambique	.mz
Kyrgyz Republic	.kg	Myanmar	.mm
Laos	.la	Namibia	.na
Latvia	.lv	Nauru	.nr
Lebanon	.lb	Nepal	.np
Lesotho	.ls	Netherland Antilles	.an
Liberia	.lr	Netherlands	.nl
Libya	.ly	New Caledonia (Fr.)	.nc
Liechtenstein	.li	New Zealand	.nz
Lithuania	.lt	Nicaragua	.ni
Luxembourg	.lu	Niger	.ne
Macau	.mo	Nigeria	.ng
Macedonia	.mk	Niue	.nu
Madagascar, Republic of	.mg	Norfolk Island	.nf
Malawi	.mw	Northern Mariana Isl.	.mp
Malaysia	.my	Norway	.no
Maldives	.mv	Oman	.om
Mali	.ml	Pakistan	.pk
Malta	.mt	Palau	.pw

Panama	.pa	Spain	.es
Papua New Guinea	.pg	Sri Lanka	.lk
Paraguay	.py	St. Helena	.sh
Peru	.pe	St. Pierre & Miquelon	.pm
Philippines	.ph	St. Tome & Principe	.st
Pitcairn	.pn	St. Kitts & Nevis	.kn
Poland	.pl	St. Vincent & Grenadines	.vc
Polynesia (Fr.)	.pf	Sudan	.sd
Portugal	.pt	Suriname	.sr
Puerto Rico	.pr	Svalbard & Jan Mayen Is	.sj
Qatar	.qa	Swaziland	.sz
Reunion	.re	Sweden	.se
Romania	.ro	Switzerland	.ch
Russian Federation	.ru	Syria	.sy
Rwanda	.rw	Tadjikistan	.tj
Saint Lucia	.lc	Taiwan	.tw
Samoa	.ws	Tanzania	.tz
San Marino	.sm	Thailand	.th
Saudi Arabia	.sa	Togo	.tg
Senegal	.sn	Tokelau	.tk
Seychelles	.sc	Tonga	.to
Sierra Leone	.sl	Trinidad & Tobago	.tt
Singapore	.sg	Tunisia	.tn
Slovakia (Slovak Rep)	.sk	Turkey	.tr
Slovenia	.si	Turkmenistan	.tm
Solomon Islands	.sb	Turks & Caicos Islands	.tc
Somalia	.so	Tuvalu	.tv
South Africa	.za	Uganda	.ug
South Georgia &		Ukraine	.ua
South Sandwich Islands	.gs	United Arab Emirates	.ae
Soviet Union	.su	United Kingdom	.uk

United States	.us
Uruguay	.uy
US Minor outlying Isl.	.um
Uzbekistan	.uz
Vanuatu	.vu
Vatican City State	.va
Venezuela	.ve
Vietnam	.vn
Virgin Islands (British)	.vg
Virgin Islands (US)	.vi
Wallis & Futuna Islands	.wf
Western Sahara	.eh
Yemen	.ye
Yugoslavia	.yu
Zaire	.zr
Zambia	.zm
Zimbabwe	.zw

INDEX

COLOPHON

This book was developed on a Macintosh Quadra 650. All pages were produced in Aldus PageMaker 5.0. Some graphics were produced or edited using Adobe Illustrator 5.0. Chapter titles are set in Anna. The body text is Palatino with Futura subheads, sidebars and tables. The title of the book (on the cover and title pages) is set in Michelangelo. Page proofs were output to a Hewlett-Packard LaserJet 4M Plus and final film output was produced using a Linotronic 330.

NOTES

NOTES

NOTES

Insightful Guides

Voodoo Mac, Second Edition

$24.95, 464 pages, illustrated

Whether you're a power user looking for new shortcuts or a beginner trying to make sense of it all, *Voodoo Mac* has something for everyone! Computer veteran Kay Nelson has compiled hundreds of invaluable tips, tricks, hints and shortcuts that simplify your Macintosh tasks and save time—including disk and drive magic, font and printing tips, alias alchemy and more! The companion disk contains shareware, utilities and fonts to help Mac users master their machines.

The System 7.5 Book, Third Edition

$24.95, 736 pages, illustrated

The bestselling book on System 7, now revised, updated and re-titled! *The System 7.5 Book* is the industry's recognized standard and the last word on the Macintosh and PowerMac operating systems. Includes a complete overview of AppleHelp, AOCE, e-mail, fax, PC Exchange, MacTCP, QuickTime and more!

Looking Good in Print, Third Edition

$24.95, 464 pages, illustrated

For use with any software or hardware, this desktop design bible has become the standard among novice and experienced desktop publishers alike. Now with more than 300,000 copies in print, *Looking Good in Print, Third Edition,* is even better—including new sections on photography and scanning. Learn the fundamentals of professional-quality design along with tips on resources and reference materials.

Voodoo Windows
$19.95, 312 pages, illustrated

Work Windows wizardry with productivity-enhancing tips. Organized by subject, this book offers a wealth of Windows techniques, shortcuts and never-before-published tricks that will streamline your daily tasks and save time. A great reference for beginners and experienced users alike.

The Windows Shareware 500
$39.95, 456 pages, illustrated

The best Windows shareware available, from thousands of contenders. Includes utilities, sounds, fonts, icons, games, clip art, multimedia and more. **BONUS:** Four companion disks: three that feature top-rated programs and an America Online membership disk. Includes 10 hours free online time (for new members only)!

The Visual Guide to Visual Basic for Windows, Second Edition
$29.95, 1282 pages, illustrated

An A-to-Z examination of every command and technique in Microsoft's landmark GUI language, including functions, illustrations and suggested uses for each. Fully updated for Version 3.0, it offers users at all levels insight on customizing Windows and creating useful applications that look professional and perform efficiently. With more than 600 illustrations, it is truly the classic reference for Microsoft's bestselling language.

Internet Resources

The Internet Tour Guides, Second Editions

Mac Edition: $29.95, 432 pages, illustrated
Windows Edition: $29.95, 416 pages, illustrated

Users can now navigate the Internet the easy way: by pointing and clicking, dragging and dropping. In easy-to-read, entertaining prose, the *Internet Tour Guides* lead you through installing and using the software enclosed in the book to send and receive e-mail, transfer files, search the Internet's vast resources and more! **BONUS**: Free trial access and two free electronic updates.

Mosaic Quick Tours

Mac Edition: $12.00, 208 pages, illustrated
Windows Edition: $12.00, 216 pages, illustrated

The *Mosaic Quick Tours* introduce the how-to's of hypertext travel in a picturesque guide. Mosaic™, the "killer app" of the Internet, lets you view linked text, audio and video resources thousands of miles apart. Learn to use Mosaic for all your information hunting—including Gopher searches, newsgroup reading and file transfers via FTP.

Walking the World Wide Web

$29.95, 361 pages, illustrated

Enough of lengthy listings! This tour features more than 300 memorable Web sites, with in-depth descriptions of what's special about each. Includes international sites, exotic exhibits, entertainment, business and more. The companion CD-ROM contains Ventana Mosaic™ and a hyperlinked version of the book, providing live links when you log on to the Internet.

Internet Virtual Worlds Quick Tour
$14.00, 150 pages, illustrated

Learn to locate and master real-time interactive communication forums and games by participating in the virtual worlds of MUD (Multi-User Dimension) and MOO (Mud Object-Oriented). *Internet Virtual Worlds Quick Tour* introduces users to the basic functions by defining different categories (individual, interactive and both) and detailing standard protocols. Also revealed is the insider's lexicon of these mysterious cyberworlds. Available March 1995.

Internet Roadside Attractions
$29.95, 376 pages, illustrated

Why take the word of one when you can get a quorum? Seven experienced Internauts—teachers and bestselling authors—share their favorite Web sites, Gophers, FTP sites, chats, games, newsgroups and mailing lists. Organized alphabetically by category for easy browsing with in-depth descriptions. The companion CD-ROM contains the entire text of the book, hyperlinked for off-line browsing and online Web hopping.

Internet Chat Quick Tour
$14.00, 150 pages, illustrated

Global conversations in real-time are an integral part of the Internet. The worldwide chat network is where users find online help and forums on the latest scientific research. The *Internet Chat Quick Tour* describes the best software sites for users to chat on a variety of subjects and shows users where to take out verbal aggression. Available March 1995.

 Books marked with this logo include a free Internet *Online Companion*™, featuring archives of free utilities plus a software archive and links to other Internet resources.

TITLE	ISBN	Quantity	Price		Total
Voodoo Mac, 2nd Edition	1-56604-177-5	_____	x $24.95	=	$_____
The System 7.5 Book, 3rd Edition	1-56604-129-5	_____	x $24.95	=	$_____
Looking Good in Print, 3rd Edition	1-56604-047-7	_____	x $24.95	=	$_____
Voodoo Windows	1-56604-005-1	_____	x $19.95	=	$_____
The Windows Shareware 500	1-56604-045-0	_____	x $39.95	=	$_____
The Visual Guide to Visual Basic for Windows, 2nd Edition	1-56604-063-9	_____	x $29.95	=	$_____
The Mac Internet Tour Guide, 2nd Edition	1-56604-173-2	_____	x $29.95	=	$_____
The Windows Internet Tour Guide, 2nd Edition	1-56604-174-0	_____	x $29.95	=	$_____
Mosaic Quick Tour for Mac	1-56604-195-3	_____	x $12.00	=	$_____
Mosaic Quick Tour for Windows	1-56604-194-5	_____	x $12.00	=	$_____
Walking the World Wide Web	1-56604-208-9	_____	x $29.95	=	$_____
Internet Virtual Worlds Quick Tour	1-56604-222-4	_____	x $14.00	=	$_____
Internet Roadside Attractions	1-56604-193-7	_____	x $29.95	=	$_____
Internet Chat Quick Tour	1-56604-223-2	_____	x $14.00	=	$_____
Internet E-Mail Quick Tour	1-56604-220-8	_____	x $14.00	=	$_____

To order any Ventana Press title, complete this order form and mail or fax it to us, with payment, for quick shipment.

Subtotal = $_____

Shipping = $_____

TOTAL = $_____

SHIPPING:

For all standard orders, please ADD $4.50/first book, $1.35/each additional.
For "two-day air," ADD $8.25/first book, $2.25/each additional.
For orders to Canada, ADD $6.50/book.
For orders sent C.O.D., ADD $4.50 to your shipping rate.
North Carolina residents must ADD 6% sales tax.
International orders require additional shipping charges.

Name _____ Telephone _____

Company _____

Address (No PO Box) _____

City _____ State _____ Zip _____

____ Payment enclosed ____ VISA ____ MC Acc't # _____ Exp. Date _____

Exact name on card _____ Signature _____

Mail to: Ventana Press, PO Box 2468, Chapel Hill, NC 27515 ☎ 800/743-5369 Fax 919/942-1140